LISTEN TO ME
A CHILD'S PLEA

CARL·DAVID·ANDERSON

Andrew Benzie Books
Walnut Creek, California

Published by Andrew Benzie Books
www.andrewbenziebooks.com

Copyright © 2017 Carl David Anderson
All rights reserved.

No part of this publication may be reproduced, distributed or transmitted in any form or by any means, or stored in a database or retrieval system without prior written permission of the author.

Printed in the United States of America

Second Edition: August 2018

10 9 8 7 6 5 4 3 2

ISBN 978-1-941713-58-7

In order to preserve my friends' and students' privacy, certain names have been changed.

Cover design by Carl David Anderson, created by Andrew Benzie
Book design by Andrew Benzie

This book is for:

my mother and father, my first teachers;

all of my students, who hopefully survived my
well-intentioned ideas, experiments, and many
mistakes without too much damage;

the parents of my students,
for entrusting me with your most precious treasure;

those who have been labeled,
written off, ignored, put-down;

those who have been treated differently
for reasons not of your making;

And for those, young and old, without a voice.

As a primary teacher for about 35 years, I went through a continuum of "ability stages," from CLUELESS, to FUNCTIONING, eventually arriving at COMPETENT ENOUGH. Hopefully, this book, LISTEN TO ME: A Child's Plea, will help the "novice" teacher shorten this often lengthy learning curve, avoid some of the common pitfalls, and minimize the "wheel problems," spinning your wheels and reinventing the wheel. With this in mind, I've included:

- Ideas and projects which support the new teacher, especially in the primary grades
- Things I wish I had known when I entered the classroom on the first day of school
- Thoughts on addressing THE "OTHER" BASICS such as SELF-ESTEEM and COMMUNICATION
- What your students want you to know

TABLE OF CONTENTS

A Child's Plea i
A Personal Perspective iii
Introduction v
1 A Long Time Ago 1
2 Enlightenment 9
3 My First Class 11
4 Confronting My Past 15
5 Planning for the Year 17
6 The First Day 23
7 The "Other" Basics 33
8 Discipline 41
9 Friendship 49
10 Positive Thinking 53
11 Listening to Kids 59
12 Character Education 67
13 Disabilities 69
14 Bullying 73
15 Glossophobia 77
16 Reading 83
17 Math 95
18 Writing 99
19 Arts and Music 109
20 You Might Consider 113
21 Hand Work 121
22 The Team 129

23	Stigmas	145
24	A Few of My Students	153
25	Every Four Years	163
26	Mapping the World by Heart	167
27	All Varieties	169
28	Privileged	171
29	History Month	173
30	A Right or a Privilege	175
31	Young Philosophers	179
32	The Children Know	181
33	Words Matter	183
34	Pearls of Wisdom	185
35	Controversies	191
36	Acronyms	201
37	Wouldn't It Be Great If	203
38	Some Encouraging Words	205
39	Marbles	207
40	One of the Biggest Compliments	209
41	World's Greatest	211
42	Other Inspirational Quotes	213
43	Reflections	215
44	Caution!	217
	Acknowledgements	219
	About the Author	221

A CHILD'S PLEA

I am a child. I am smaller, and have been on this planet for fewer years, so I may lack your wisdom, but I have the same basic needs:

I want to be respected, listened to, and treated the same as others. No worse or no better because of the color of my skin, my gender, last name, birth place, religion, beliefs of my family, our socio-economic status, or the language we speak.

If you judge me, do so by criteria over which I have control: my words, actions, conduct, ideas, and character.

If I have a physical, mental, emotional, or learning challenge, don't be afraid of me, and please don't write me off.

Every person has special needs; I assume you will do what is best for each of us. Be patient, believe in me, and encourage me to reach my potential.

Like everyone, I have strengths. Assist me in identifying and nurturing these so that I may utilize my gifts and talents, and share them with others. Work with me on my weaknesses so that they may become strengths. Teach me the skills I require to compensate for any "deficiencies" as I strive for this goal.

If I misbehave, I could be crying out for help; something might be bothering me. I may be concerned or worried about some unresolved aspect of my life, at home, school, or elsewhere. It is possible that I am just bored and not being challenged.

I listen to what you say, and what you don't say, learning from your words and actions that you consciously, and unconsciously, model for me. I gather this input that I hear, observe, and read, and filter it through my values, reason, and common sense, to form my unique belief system.

I trust you to protect and defend me from dangers, bullying, and unfair treatment at the school site, as well as from put-downs and sarcasm within the classroom.

Help me feel safe so I have the confidence to be me, free to express my thoughts and ideas.

Be my advocate; show me that you care, help me feel good about myself, and I will do my best to be a good student, on my journey to becoming a responsible, contributing member of society.

I expect the same treatment for my classmates and friends. What you do to them, you do to me.

This preamble to LISTEN TO ME: A Child's Plea, encapsulates the wishes, dreams, frustrations, the pleas I have heard from my students and other children over the years. It also embraces the experiences and insights of countless adults (former children), and expresses what they wish they could have said to their teachers and other adults.

It contains components which might be included in a children's bill of rights, a document which could be hung in every classroom and revisited periodically.

A PERSONAL PERSPECTIVE

I made the decision to quit my teaching job to become a caregiver, transitioning from advocating for young children to advocating for older adults, altering my reading list from brain research and children's rights to The New England Journal of Medicine and patients' rights. This was an easier adjustment than one may think as both professions involve assisting those who are frequently without a voice.

Often in the middle of the night or in the emergency room, as a diversion from my responsibilities, I began jotting down (mostly) illegible notes, chronicling my career in education. These documents recounted my own childhood experiences as well as my decades in the classroom. Eventually, I would accumulate an abundance of WORD files, thoughts which came to me in a dream or on an early morning meditative walk.

Initially, I was not concerned with how others might perceive these recollections as they were intended solely for my personal use. They contained my observations, reasoning, truth, and reality as I perceived it. I eliminated the accurate but more controversial accounts, narrowing down the files to those which might be beneficial to a new teacher, or anyone interested in the education of children.

I began hearing that I should consider sharing this narrative with others. My initial response was **absolutely not**. This was too personal for me. My greatest concern was that I might expose the identities, the life stories, of some of my students. Their privacy was more important to me than any benefits which might be reaped by another person.

When I chose to listen to this advice, and started interpreting my archive into an informal dialog for young teachers, I worried that one of my former students (or another reader) might take some of this information **too** personally. They might think they "see" themselves, particularly in the sections relating to self-esteem, and become upset. It is easy to lose sight of the reality that the vast majority of us have some "issue," need, or fear which keeps us from reaching our full potential. I decided to include these sections in the book because I believe that these factors, which often affect one's mental health, are ubiquitous in our society. If they are not addressed (preferably at an early age), they could be detrimental to an individual, possibly impact their ability to achieve, to soar, and could ultimately erode the foundations of our society, our civilization.

A teacher should possess enough information about each student to understand their unique circumstances, while avoiding over-analyzing them. Dwelling on these issues can make a child (or anyone) feel that they are somehow flawed, damaged, imperfect, or that they are being judged. Help the child understand that they are not controlled, limited, or defined by their experiences or their situation.

Each child comes with their own "set of instructions." If one **really** listens, and is mindful of the **whole** child, the child will often reveal the missing piece(s) which completes their unique jigsaw puzzle.

INTRODUCTION

Contrary to what some believe, education does not begin in high school. The problems and challenges that many adolescents face don't all begin in their teens. With few exceptions, they don't all of a sudden become bored, burned-out, turned off, frustrated, withdrawn, depressed, angry, or feel worthless, unworthy, that all is hopeless. For many individuals, these negative feelings, thoughts, emotions can be traced back to their early experiences in school.

While children are hopefully building a strong foundation in the academic basics of reading, math, language, and writing, we should also be introducing them to, and modeling, OTHER BASICS. We should be providing them with tools which prepare them to function in the world they live in, and arming them with a protective coat of armor so that they can better survive the challenges of life.

Among these "OTHER" BASICS are empathy and tolerance, respect for themselves and others, the arts of listening and communication, taking responsibility, and understanding the concept of cause and effect. But possibly the greatest gift that we can give each child, one that can literally change their life, is a contribution to their self-esteem, a boost in their confidence.

"Self-esteem isn't anything," rebutted one of my administrators, a remark for which I'd give her partial credit. SELF-ESTEEM ISN'T *ANYTHING*, IT'S **EVERYTHING**!

We should be taking advantage in these early years when children are naturally curious, enthusiastic, trusting, and eager to learn, to infuse the classrooms with all of the resources at our disposal. This should include not only adequate financial support but also the collective knowledge and expertise of the educators at the school site, in the school district, and from around the world, utilizing current research, time-proven and creative solutions, and common sense.

When we could be getting the best "bang for the buck," we should be targeting, diagnosing, and addressing the students' academic, emotional, and other needs, not quitting until we have discovered the missing puzzle piece(s) which make each of them whole.

Too often we fail to diagnose, or we misdiagnose a problem, give up on a child, ignore or camouflage our failures and defer them to the future, hoping that someone else will "fix" them. We often conform to a school or district policy which does not allow for diagnosis or testing until a child is (fill in the blank) years below grade level, at which time he or she is way behind their classmates, frustrated, defeated, and has lost much of their enthusiasm, confidence, self-esteem, and hope. The solution is too often to give them more and more of what isn't working, or maybe retain them, even though we are not sure how to help them. If we fail to address their academic or emotional needs at this age, we will pay dearly later on.

I am going to reveal a little secret. It is often amazingly simple to turn a young child around, set them on the right path, give them a chance at a better life. I have frequently heard iterations on the retort "YEH, IT'S EASY FOR YOU, YOU WORK WITH LITTLE KIDS!" My point exactly!

You've heard the lament, "IF ONLY I KNEW THEN WHAT I KNOW NOW!"—In this book, LISTEN TO ME: A Child's Plea, I offer ideas, projects, suggestions, which have worked for me in the first, second, and third grades. These are things I wish I had known when I began teaching, things which would have made my life, and the lives of my students, so much better and easier.

I make no claims that these views are the answer to the world's problems, or that they will cure what ails the American education system. There is obviously not just one way, and these methods may not be the best way for you and your young learners. You will discover that for yourself.

"I ain't lookin' for you to feel like me, see like me, or be like me."
— Dylan

That said, if I can shorten the learning curve for a young teacher, administrator, or parent, if one is inspired to attempt a new idea or approach, reads a passage which causes them to think, rethink, or affirm a belief, gets them excited, angry, or motivated, my labor will not have been in vain.

Nobody Was More Surprised

Nobody was more surprised than me when I became a "teacher." Except for a short period when I considered law school in order to be an advocate for women, I had "always" assumed that I would study architecture.

Since I was a child, I have enjoyed PLAYING with younger kids, whether it was getting down on all fours and riding my relatives around the house, racing them down a grocery store aisle in a shopping cart, or playing peek-a-boo with a bored toddler during a church sermon. Later, when I was more mature and sophisticated, I would graduate to performing in restaurants, where I would entertain a child in the adjacent booth. While the adults were involved in conversation, I would adorn my face with colorful food items: broccoli in the ears, a pair of green beans protruding from my nostrils, a ketchup-laden french-fry mustache, a carrot cigar, and conclude the effect with a wiggle of my eyebrows. My altered physiognomy would be disassembled in time for the inevitable squeal, "MOMMY, MOMMY, LOOK AT THAT MAN!" and the response, "Don't bother that nice man, he's trying to eat!" I would give a slight nod and a smile which let them know that I understood, no problem.

But teaching in a classroom with 30 plus kids never entered my mind, not consciously. Looking back, my assumptions, decisions, planning, were possibly for naught. My career "choice" appears to have been guided by an external source. I feel that my "purpose in life" was orchestrated from an early age by an "invisible hand." "Yeh, right," you're probably saying. I don't blame you.

My earliest memory is difficult to put into words. When I was very young, two or possibly three, I experienced this overwhelming "feeling" which left me with a clear sense of what would be important in my life, that EVERY PERSON MATTERS. I have tried, unsuccessfully, to recover the intensity of this initial sensation, to determine its genesis, but the message inhabits me and has been a driving force in my educational philosophies, as well as my daily life, affecting my thoughts and opinions on just about all issues.

1   A LONG TIME AGO
(My Own Experience)

"Those who tell their own story, you know, must be listened to with caution."
— Jane Austen

Way before children were expected to read shortly after exiting the womb, I attended kindergarten. At that time, the emphasis was on "socialization." We never got tired of the outdoor playground equipment, and indoors we played with blocks, took naps though we weren't the least bit sleepy, ate graham crackers and drank milk even when we were still full from having just eaten lunch at home. I already knew how to read and was disappointed that we weren't learning new stuff like my older brother was. Still, I enjoyed school… up until that one day in June. The kindergarten year was coming to an end, it was the last week before summer vacation. My classmates and I were excited because we would be visiting the three first grade classrooms to see what we would be doing in the fall when we began "real school."

Two of the teachers seemed nice, and their proud "almost second graders" explained some of the things they had learned during the year. The third teacher frowned at us while leading her children in the chant, "Kindergarten Baby, Born in the Gravy." Most of us didn't think it was funny and some were upset. We learned from the older kids that this teacher was known as "The Witch."

To this day, when I hear the word "witch," I visualize this woman. Occasionally that summer, I would worry that I might end up in her room.

MRS. POND

I did not get my first or second choice. On a positive note, if I had, I probably would not have become a teacher, and would not be writing this book, which could be sub-titled MOST OF WHAT I NEEDED TO KNOW TO TEACH THE PRIMARY GRADES, I LEARNED IN FIRST GRADE.

I was unhappy when I saw my name on Mrs. Pond's list, but my mom would have consoled me and convinced me that it would be all right, and it was, up until the first rain of the season, sometime in September.

Released from incarceration, being six-year old boys, my friend A.H. and I were drawn to the first suitable mud puddle, where we literally jumped right in. We were in pig heaven until A's mother arrived. Determining that I, and not her angel, had been the instigator, she grabbed my arm and dragged me to our classroom where Mrs. Pond shook her head in disgust, questioning neither of us, and pointed in the direction of the principal's office. I somehow endured the agonizing wait (long enough to ensure that I would simmer in my guilt) outside his office. When we were finally allowed to enter his domain, the principal gave the requisite look which we knew meant, shame on you. Again, neither A nor I were asked to tell our story. Since I was to blame, my (first) punishment was to clean A off using paper towels from the dispenser, and then I was to apologize to him, and "mean it," which to me meant that I should say I was sorry for something I hadn't done!

I accepted this without complaint, believing that this would get me out of there and on my way home. Unfortunately, we were not through. "SHOULD WE CALL YOUR MOTHER AND TELL HER WHAT YOU'VE DONE?"

This was rhetorical as he had already dialed my home number, and was beginning to talk with my mother. I listened to what he told her which had little semblance to the truth. I was stressed and humiliated, but my biggest concern was that my parents would be upset, and I would not have done anything to hurt them!

Fortunately, two adults that day took the time to listen to me. My parents listened to my version, and believed me. Two other times while I was in elementary school they would hear of my visits to this principal, but by then they would have greater knowledge of him, his methods, and so would take everything he said with a grain of salt.

As much as possible I got into a routine in the prison-like environment of Mrs. Pond's classroom. She continued to barrage us with ditto work sheets, a seemingly endless supply for every subject. I knew how to read, and was apparently proficient enough in basic math, so I would complete these tasks quickly and then be expected to sit quietly for the remainder of the hour with no additional busy work or challenge. Since there were no other viable options, I would frequently invent mind games, but more often I would observe the interactions between the "adult in the room" and my classmates, my friends.

I never did get comfortable with this scary woman. I would do my work and try to be well-behaved. If you were able to keep up with the dittos, and didn't cause any problems (remained quiet) you were usually relatively safe from her wrath. If you were bored, you were ignored. Those unfortunate to struggle with any of the "curriculum" would be assaulted with her biting sarcasm, cheap shots, and put-downs. Over the year, one could witness the gradual chipping away of these children's confidence. This was the "sink or swim" philosophy on steroids, as utilized by a sick person who shouldn't have been allowed anywhere near kids.

Occasionally, I would be pulled out to read a paragraph, or asked to read a passage for a minute (fluency). I was able to read rapidly for a short duration, so no one was aware that I would get very tired when I read for any length of time and would therefore refrain from reading. I also discovered on my own that it was often difficult for me to focus on what I was reading as I would venture off on some exciting tangent or journey.

I learned very little academically in first grade, but I did come away with the understanding that the adults at this school were not going to listen to me.

A MORE PLEASANT YEAR

Second grade would prove to be a more pleasant, but frustrating year. I can't put faces to the two seemingly nice young teachers assigned to our class that year, one on the first day of school, and one about half-way through the year, but I've always remembered their names. Mrs. W and Mrs. K were both "with child," and soon left us. A colleague who taught there during this period informed me that they were both young, brand new teachers and were never heard from again. It seemed that whenever we got comfortable or became fond of a teacher, they would desert us. "Experts" claim that children are flexible, and that these stressful situations do not bother us all that much, that we recover quickly.

It was another school year when I learned little and would have an abundance of time to think and observe. Although there was little consistency in the instruction, and not a lot of help for those who found the curriculum challenging, I don't remember any of the adults being mean.

We had many substitutes that year, but only one was memorable to me. "You'll never guess my name!" she challenged us. "MRS. TWEED!" I blurted out.

I believe that she fainted, as she appeared to melt like candle wax. I would later cut out an obituary as evidence that she had existed, was indeed a real person, and not a figment of my imagination.

I won the school spelling bee that year, but instead of being thrilled or proud, I was troubled. I had a fear of being onstage. Also, I was afraid that no one would listen to me when I attempted to tell them that I had won unfairly. I had stared at that exact word that very morning at the breakfast table, on the front page of my dad's newspaper... COMMUNIQUÉ.

Many students struggled that year, at least partially because of the numerous adults who never stayed that long. Had the curriculum been more challenging, I could have been one of those struggling children.

Many of the substitute teachers seemed oblivious, or ignored, that my classmate was having difficulties with reading. It was the first time that I would offer to help another student academically. Evidently, somewhere along the line this deficiency was remedied, or compensated for, as the last I heard he was doing WELL!

Report card day was a big occasion in our household. We would celebrate our hard work by going out for a banana split, quite a treat for us. My second-grade final report was kind of a shocker to the members of my family. There were two Cs, the only ones I would receive until high school chemistry, when I "forgot" to turn in any homework. ART and HANDWRITING! Those who know me would recognize these as possibly my greatest strengths. I explained to my parents that we never had art (I can't recall a single art lesson in my entire elementary, middle school, or high school education), and that several of the substitutes had asked me to write on the chalkboard because they said I had "nice" handwriting.

As would become tradition, I also received a "check" in the "average" space (C) for self-control. Evidently, while sitting there with nothing to do, I had resorted to talking with my neighbors. And then there was the now familiar notation in the "comments" section, "He only does the bare minimum." I never failed to complete an assignment, always to the best of my ability. Perhaps I was expected to create my own curriculum.

It was decided, against the protests of my parents, that I would be "double-promoted" to the fourth grade. According to my mother, they were afraid that I would otherwise begin to disrupt the class.

MORE OF THE SAME

Fourth grade was more of the same, more dittos and more mind games as we were again on our own once we finished our work. I did become more skilled at speaking to my neighbors without getting caught. Our teacher, dubbed "Heartless H" by many, wasn't what anyone would call nice, didn't garner much respect, and she didn't appear to be too fond of kids, but it could have been much worse.

We did have plenty of opportunities to practice our handwriting and creative writing, at least the boys did. This was a time when kids (mainly boys) played marbles at every opportunity... in the gutters to and from school, at recess, especially the long one after lunch. Each day we faced a dilemma. We never knew when the bell would ring, but when it did we were required to freeze until we heard the next one which meant to line up immediately. Upon entering the classroom, our hands were inspected for dirt. If found to be one of the unwashed, we would be scolded and given a piece of paper upon which we were required to pen a note to our parents admitting our transgression. Since this happened almost every day, the kids, and our parents, eventually refused to take it seriously.

This was the year that I would make my second visit to the principal's office. While waiting in line to play tetherball, I heard someone remark to one of the players, L.L., "We're going to burn your heart out, and then you'll die!" I was considered guilty because I was in the vicinity of the crime. The kids and the parents knew that it was futile to attempt to defend oneself against charges by the principal, to expect that we might be listened to, let alone expect justice, so we simply accepted our sentence, a week of lunch recesses on the bench.

Despite her idiosyncrasies, we were loyal to Mrs. H, and never disclosed to our parents her need for "medication." Surprisingly, she was always much nicer after she took the occasional sip from the bottle in that brown paper bag.

THE ONE TEACHER

In fifth grade, I met the one elementary school teacher who would have a positive influence on my life, Miss T, my music teacher. I can still visualize the class putting our heads down and listening to the recording of "Peter and the Wolf," but it was the day she cued up "The Carnival of the Animals" by Camille Saint-Saens that music made a permanent mark on my world. Hearing "The Swan," "normally played by the cello, but this time played on the double-bass," I could feel every cell in my body awakening. I don't know if it was my facial expression, the goose bumps, or the tears that tipped her off, but at a later session she whispered that she brought a recording that she thought I might enjoy. "The Swan," played by cellist Pablo Casals, was one of the most beautiful pieces of music I had (have) ever heard. It penetrated my soul.

When Miss T heard that I would be taking trumpet lessons in the school music program, she invited me to hear a world-famous trumpet player who was visiting the symphony in which she played the clarinet. Miss T cared about me and other children as unique individuals, and was not only willing, but interested in listening to us kids.

NATO

My last year of elementary school, sixth grade, would mark my third one-way conversation with our principal. While digesting the Weekly Reader, I became intrigued by an article about NATO. As an 11-year-old, I thought it pretty cool that countries would stick up for one another. Why couldn't this work in our school? I discussed this with three of my friends who concurred that this might be just what the kids at our school needed.

We let it be known that we would be providing a service for those who were being picked on, mistreated by an adult or another child, or who just wanted to talk. Soon other sixth graders asked to join the ranks. It proved so popular that some fifth graders approached us wanting to launch an auxiliary group. In my recollection, it was an especially peaceful, harmonious year.

One day towards the end of the year, we watched the principal approach our classroom door and motion to our teacher, who nodded to me. In his office, the principal informed me that he was perfectly capable of "controlling" the school and that NATO would disband immediately. PERIOD. NO DISCUSSION. It was explained to me by my teacher that some fourth-graders who had adopted the name of our "club," were fighting on the way home from school.

About twenty years later I related this account to a high-ranking NATO official, in Louvain, Belgium, which earned a hearty laugh and led to a fascinating conversation.

*"In the little world in which children have their existence...
there is nothing so finely perceived and so finely felt,
as injustice."*
— Charles Dickens in Great Expectations

No, this wasn't the idyllic, nurturing early-childhood educational experience that many have, that *you* may have had. Innumerable people I've talked to, those with far more horrific stories, would have been overjoyed to trade places with me. I am not complaining. My experiences served me well later when I was figuring things out, when I was learning how to, and **HOW NOT TO** teach.

2   ENLIGHTENMENT

I gained much enlightenment from my early job experiences. My first paying jobs, mowing lawns, watering and house-sitting for neighbors on vacation, taught me responsibility. Delivering newspapers at age eleven, I discovered that there were some scary dogs out there, and some even scarier people. One high school job taught me that if you were part of a well-run organization, where all worked towards a common goal and produced a superior product, you could be successful.

For one very long week during summer break, a friend and I attempted what would prove to be the hardest (physical) job I would ever have. Bending over for eight grueling hours in the sun to pick tomatoes was back-breaking, torturous, with little financial gain at the end of the week. Ironically, the other workers, uncomplaining and seemingly indefatigable men, women and children, almost all from a neighboring country, were stereotyped as LAZY, which was ludicrous. They were said to be stealing jobs from other Americans, but at least during that week we labored, the two of us were the only "Americans" to apply.

At a summer job during college, I was offended by the amount of waste I perceived. I was astonished when, while watching the evening news, I listened to a government representative assuring the public that we were NOT DOING what I HAD BEEN DOING that day.

Another summer job which I held concurrently confirmed that some could be denied membership to "the club" because of the color of their skin or their religion.

Despite my varied experiences, college courses, and teacher's training, I was ill-prepared for what was to come.

3 MY FIRST CLASS

It was my choice to teach at an "at risk" school, one which was saturated with state and federal funding, got top priority in the bussing schedule, and was considered a "tough" school. "You don't want to teach there," was the gratuitous advice I received from the personnel director after I declined another position that "any educator would lust after." "YES," I responded, "I DO."

I would be teaching an "ill-conceived" first/second combination class, composed of 31 students.

The first few minutes of my first day would be a preview of what was in store for me. As I was welcoming my students, a first grader, for an unknown reason, threw a punch and knocked out the front tooth of a second grader.

I built up the courage to call the parent of the victim at recess.

"Hi, Mrs. T, this is Mr. A, E's teacher."

"Oh, yes, Mr. A, thank you so much."

I repeated that this was E's teacher calling to say that I was sorry for what had happened this morning.

"Yes, thanks so much. E's dentist has been telling us for about a year now, 'THAT TOOTH HAS GOT TO COME OUT SOON!'"

I couldn't believe my good fortune. I remember Mrs. T fondly to this day.

I would get much insight and unsolicited advice from the parents. D's mother approached me early on, *"Mr. A, you're a nice man, but the kids are going to EAT YOU ALIVE!"* She was right.

I was so embarrassed because of my students' behavior (due to my incompetence) that I would hide-out in my room rather than visit the "teachers' lounge," and come out only when absolutely necessary. I realize now that the other teachers were probably being respectful, allowing me to figure things out for myself, giving me some space, but I felt isolated. The school had an abundance of friendly, highly-qualified educators, many of whom would probably have been happy to help had I asked. One of the wisest things a school/district can do is to assign a qualified person (ideally from the same school), one who is a good match, to mentor every new teacher.

One morning a child was being so disruptive that I moved him and his desk outside, where he proceeded to throw pebbles through the open windows (no air-conditioning because after all these were just kids). Fortunately, his arm soon got tired, or possibly he figured that he wasn't getting the attention he craved, and eventually he sheepishly entered the classroom and begged to be allowed to rejoin the class. I tried not to let on how relieved I was that he was back. Obviously, it was the wrong way to handle the situation, and I was very lucky to endure the crisis without any major repercussions such as him disappearing, breaking a window or injuring another student. Once I sent him out I had lost, at the very least, a bit of my own self-respect.

Then there was the child who earned a trip to the skating rink. He was afraid and had to be "convinced" by his mother to attend. Once he found the courage to lace up his skates and stand up, he enjoyed it so much that when it was time to leave he hid under a pinball machine, where we would finally find him an hour later. Ditto same child, on a field trip to the zoo… I forget where we eventually found him.

I managed to survive the first time a child said he hated me and called me a dog. I forgave him, even prior to noticing the small puddle of accumulated tears at his feet. I was able to respond with the words familiar to most parents, "I'm very sorry about that T, because I really like you, but you still need to finish your work."

You might be thinking that all of these anecdotes are about boys. You'd be correct, only because I had very few girls in my class that year.

As in many poorly thought-out classes, there were built-in problems. Several of the second graders commented that they felt "dumb" because they were in a "first grade class." Some of the first graders had an inflated notion of their abilities because they were in a "second grade class." Eventually some of the first graders would surpass the second graders academically, which would precipitate an erosion of self-esteem which I didn't deal with adequately.

Somehow the kids and I made it through the school year. Together, we could have written a dual-purpose survival guide, for the inexperienced, unskilled teacher, and for those children, unfortunate enough to find themselves in a classroom with this clueless teacher.

If I were given three wishes as an educator, I would use the first one to go back in time to correct the horrific mistakes that I made my first year of teaching, another chance to grant those children the nine months of quality education that they deserved.

4   CONFRONTING MY PAST

An unrelated job over the summer allowed me the time to fortify my strength and courage enough to return for a second year. As each day was becoming more manageable, rewarding, and even fun, I made the decision to deal with a part of my past which needed to be confronted lest it consciously or subconsciously affect me.

Having ascertained that my first-grade teacher had moved on but that my childhood elementary school principal had yet to be dethroned, I resolved to pay him a visit. After a particularly rewarding day I made the trek to the site where I had spent six years of my early life. I approached the secretary, explaining that I wished to speak with Mr. C. Responding to the command to enter, I stood as erect as I could and puffed out my chest in order to fill the door frame with my presence. As it turned out, the effort wasn't necessary as the man standing in front of me was not as tall as I remembered. I introduced myself as a former student who had attended this school from kindergarten through the sixth grade, and was now working as a teacher.

"Well, it's great to hear that we have turned out some successful kids!" he boasted.

"I WANTED YOU TO KNOW THAT, **BECAUSE OF YOU, I AM PRETTY SURE THAT I WILL BE A BETTER TEACHER!**"

"Wow, that's just about the nicest thing that anyone has ever said to me!"

I continued, "I WAS IN TROUBLE SEVERAL TIMES IN THIS VERY ROOM, for things of which I WAS NOT GUILTY. You would have known that, HAD YOU LISTENED TO ME! Instead, you EMBARRASSED AND HUMILIATED ME and many of my friends and classmates! You robbed many of them of their self-worth and confidence, along with their respect for, and trust of, adults, THE VERY PEOPLE ON WHOM THEY SHOULD BE ABLE TO DEPEND.

Because of my experiences at this school, I PLEDGE THAT I WILL MAKE EVERY EFFORT TO LISTEN TO **ALL** OF MY STUDENTS, AND NOT PRE-JUDGE THEM. I WILL SHOW EACH OF THEM THE RESPECT THAT THEY DESERVE."

He appeared to be stunned, and one could hear the proverbial pin drop as I left the room.

I was able to learn from the many faux pas and near disasters of the previous year, and my second year went pretty well. Beginning teachers, don't abandon hope. Soon you will be able to laugh about that year you thought no one could possibly understand. Many more than you can imagine do empathize.

5 PLANNING FOR THE YEAR

Much of my summer "break" was spent planning for the next school year, developing (hopefully) fun, interesting, educational units, and "sponge activities" to fill in short periods of unexpected time, as well as researching ways of helping the children in my class who were experiencing learning or other challenges, the areas which were not explored in my courses or seminars, that we didn't speak about at teachers' meetings.

I normally spent the bulk of the last two or three weeks of the break in the classroom, preparing for the new class, creating bulletin boards, arranging desks, distributing materials for each student and, a tough thing for me, getting my head back into the idea of teaching. When I'm gone for too long, I immerse myself in other interests which I am unable to consider during the school year due to lack of time. Many kids have this same problem, and for this reason I am for more frequent, shorter breaks during the school year, especially for those children who tend to forget skills over long periods of unsupervised vacation.

Once the class lists were available, I sometimes visited the homes of my students, especially when I was working in neighborhoods where many members of the community feel uneasy with educators, or lack trust in the education system. I call, make an appointment, and try to visit four or five homes a day. The first reaction is often shock, disbelief, that I am willing to come to their neighborhood, meet them on their turf. If they were not comfortable with me visiting them at home, I asked them to suggest an alternate meeting place. The important thing is that we meet and talk about their child, and that we build trust, open a line of communication. Because the kids, their parents, and I had this head start, and already knew each other, we were less anxious on the first day and spent less time getting back in the groove. The years that I took the time to do this were among the most rewarding and successful.

If not a visit, you might consider writing an old-school letter, in an envelope, addressed to the parents of ___, sent by snail mail, letting the parents know how excited you are about the beginning of the new school year, and that you are looking forward to meeting and working with them and their child.

CLASSROOM ENVIRONMENT

You will want to create an environment where you and the children are comfortable, where you feel like teaching and learning for 6-7 hours a day, 5 days a week, 180 or so days a year. Since this is your home away from home, adding a little of your personality, a bit of fun, can't hurt, and just might help to inspire, motivate the kids (and you). The basics include bookcases brimming with grade level (plus some below and above level) books, good literature, some of the popular series books, biographies, poetry, science, art, including lessons on drawing. Just ask the kids, they'll be happy to make suggestions. Maybe a couple cozy, kid-sized chairs, bean bags, or an extra-thick carpet so they can relax with their new favorite book. Shelves of educational games which will buttress their thinking skills, Legos (if they promise to pick up after themselves), for when they've completed all of their assignments or the occasional "free time." Consider a few easy-care plants, or a (relatively) low-maintenance class pet. We enjoyed our Russian dwarf hamsters, which didn't smell, were fun to observe, especially when they were roaming the room in their little plastic spheres while we were cleaning their cage. They taught us about life, responsibility, and were easily transportable to children's homes for the week-ends and holidays. Perhaps you could follow through on my dream of a network (hundreds of feet) of clear plastic tubing, hanging from the ceiling at different heights, through which the creatures could circumnavigate the room at their will, providing them with needed exercise, and us with entertainment. We would all promise to take only the occasional peek, and would soon be accustomed to their movements, and remain attentive to our tasks at hand.

IN MEMORIAM

Our friend and class pet, Squeaky, passed away over the weekend. S and her family were there for her when she died, and had a small funeral service in her honor. We will miss you, Squeaky.

We have a new addition to our family. Come by when you can to meet Sonar, another Russian dwarf hamster, with her great personality and unique eyes.

If it's not a problem with your fire marshal, and you don't have a sensitive motion-sensor, I like to hang a couple wires, or fishing line, tied to hooks, from the front to the back of the room, high enough that the tallest of the children can walk beneath. These are a must for hanging artwork, keeping yarn for future projects untangled, easy access to jump ropes, or kites awaiting the perfect breeze.

My kids and I enjoyed designing and constructing a colorful, super-sized watch case and band, complete with buckle, buckle tongue, and free loops to surround the blah traditional school clock. This made it more fun to observe and monitor.

SEATING ARRANGEMENTS

I start the year in rows, with two desks pushed together to accommodate "learning buddies." Some of these partnerships will soon need to be dissolved and new ones formed which are more conducive to learning.

After we've worked with a partner for a while, we are ready to try something new. Consider letting the kids design the classroom seating arrangement. This will provide them with an additional buy-in, a part-ownership in the decision-making. We brainstorm possible designs on the board, and eventually I am able to steer (gently guide) them in the direction of a (squared-off) u-shaped arrangement facing the front of the room.

Periodically, I ask for their help in conceiving a new arrangement, one which they think will be the most beneficial (valuable) to everyone, ensure (make sure) that most children are maximizing (the greatest possible amount) their learning. I'd be amenable (open) to allowing them to sit anywhere they wanted, if it was conducive (helpful) to learning, but we must consider the custodians, make sure that we do not create a nightmare for them.

Whatever the arrangement, make allowances for those who need to move around. Provide tall tables for those who prefer to stand, and a refuge for those who occasionally need a breather from a large group situation.

The majority of them ultimately come up with some kind of array, group formation, which pleases me because I am into collaborative learning. I allow them to list a couple people who they would like to be part of their group, and try to accommodate at least one of their choices. The members will presumably have different strengths and weaknesses, will help one another, and have an equal say in decisions. If "two heads are better than one," just think how much better a team of diverse thinkers will be.

As group (cooperative) learning (I believe) is the best training for the real world, what most successful businesses and organizations subscribe to, we spend most of the remaining year in these formations. The members are rotated so that each child gets a chance to work with all of his/her classmates.

I relate it to harmonizing. It begins with an idea (a melody). Another adds to the (original) idea, with a complementary thought (harmony). As each additional voice joins in, most of the gaps are filled in (we've collaborated on solutions), and the members reach a consensus. The final product may not be what any (one) person had in mind, but most agree that it sounds pretty good.

A real benefit to the children (the singers) is that they are part of a group which has created something incredible (more than any one of them could have done alone), and that each one of them has made a significant contribution.

HINT: I've heard that cooperative learning also has benefits in certain adult situations… for instance, in a school setting, or those which involve elected representatives.

STUDENT NUMBER

Consider giving each of your students a number. It will streamline many of your chores, make your life easier, and save you lots of time. Once your class has been determined, and you have a class list in alphabetical order, simply assign each child a number in sequence.

If the student writes this number on each of their assignments, including homework, it will facilitate the collecting, and management of these papers. It takes just a minute or so first thing in the day to call the numbers (I had a classroom monitor do it), as the children will be listening, anticipating, racing, to hand in their papers. You will know immediately if someone is absent or has failed to complete the assigned task. Yes, it does put a little pressure on the students to get their work in on time. It saves you time because the papers are already in alphabetical order.

It can also be beneficial on field trips, or any time one needs to do a quick count. The children are asked to line up "by number," and one can immediately see if anyone is missing.

I sometimes give the kids a 2"x 2" square, ask them to write and decorate their number, and attach these to a shelf, so they know where to house their jump rope, yarn or some other project. The kids (and you) soon memorize all the children's numbers, everything's in order, and one can see instantly if something is amiss.

6   THE FIRST DAY

The first day of school sets the tone for the rest of the year. We were warned in education classes not to smile until Christmas. This may be good advice for one's first experience in the classroom, but my default facial expression is a smile, and this is how I choose to greet the children, along with a "good morning," on this day when most of us are at least a bit anxious. I tell them to sit anywhere they'd like. "*Anywhere?*" "Anywhere!" I say, "As long as you and the person sitting next to you can work together and help each other be better students." "*You're not going to let ___ and ___ sit next to each other, are you?*" "We'll give them a chance. If it doesn't work out I'll move them."

After everyone is seated, I welcome them to ___ grade, ask if there is anyone who is new to the school and listen to where they are from. We take attendance, checking their names against my class list, while presenting them with the name tag which I've removed from the "Welcome to ___ Grade" bulletin board. The children enjoy seeing their names written out. I tell them that I will do my best to pronounce their names correctly, but this first time they may have to help me. Do they have a nickname, one which their parents will approve of? "You already know your name, so face your name tag towards me, and I will try to learn all of your names by the end of the day."

Make sure that you don't have "extra" kids in your class that aren't on your list. There is occasionally a child who believes that no one will notice if he/she joins your class.

By now we have settled down and are ready to TCB (take care of business). If there are still parents in the room, I ask the children to say good-bye to them, and promise that we'll see them again at 3:00.

We discuss how important it is that they are present and punctual every day of the year, unless they are sick. I explain to them that (in this state) every day they are in school we get a certain amount of money, to pay for our books, teachers, electricity. If they are not here, even if they are sick, we don't receive this money.

About this time, the principal comes by to see how we are doing. I introduce him/her to the new kids, and then I turn on my concerned look. "I think we have a problem!" I tell the principal. Everyone looks at me, worry written on their faces. I continue, "There must be something wrong. Could you (the principal) please check something for me? We can't possibly have all these amazing kids in one class! This is too good to be true!" *"It's no mistake,"* the principal (hopefully) says. "Wow, this is going to be a great year!"

Next, we go over the school rules, spending more time with a first-grade class than with second or third graders since this is review for them. Then, it's off for a tour of the school, pointing out the boundaries, reinforcing the rules, and a meet and greet with some of the best people to know in the school, the plant manager, custodians, cafeteria manager, and the secretaries. If there is time, we might take a quick run/jog/walk lap around the field, and then back to the classroom.

Since this is their classroom as well as mine, (to give them ownership) we decide together what the classroom rules should be. While discussing the need for rules, I allow them to experience the chaos which would prevail if we had none or ignored them. I let them yell, walk around the room, shout out, whatever (within reason), for about 10 seconds (It will appear longer), and then cut it off with a slicing motion of my hand. They are laughing but quickly understand the reason for guidelines. "What rules do you think we need, so we're not out of control, can learn as much as possible, make it to the next grade, and I can keep my job?"

By first grade, definitely by second, they are well-versed in the basic rules, and by third, I fill up two large white boards with their suggestions. I say, "Wow, that's a lot of rules! I can't think of any which you've missed, but there are too many to write on a chart. Do you think we can cut these down a bit? What do you think about these?" Respect yourself and others. Don't keep the teacher from teaching or your classmates from learning. Do your best.

I challenge them to look through their impressive, comprehensive, LONG list to see if there are any which wouldn't be covered by our more manageable, shorter list. After a few questions, comments, we agree to give these a try, we can always add more later if necessary. Before we are excused for recess, buddies are assigned for all of the kids who are new to the school.

After the break, we consider the next step in the process of classroom management, the behavior plan. I confide in them that I must turn in a plan to the principal which includes the consequences, what will happen to them if they can't follow the rules. "We may never need to use it with **this** group, but it's a rule which I must follow."

You probably have a discipline plan in mind which works for you, your personality, your philosophies. If left to the children, they inevitably come up with some iteration of the "turn your card over" plan. As they suggest this, I detect dyspeptic looks, sad faces, and groans. Even so, we decide to try it.

Within a week or two it is clear that the majority of the kids are not happy with this discipline plan, and when we open it for discussion, they plead with me to disband it. "Are you sure?" They are (I am relieved). "All right, if you think that we can do without it, I will trust your judgment. It will be our official plan, the one which we will give to the principal and your parents. If we later find that we need it, we may have to return to it."

I don't tell them that, except on rare occasions, I do not send kids to the principal for negative, DISCIPLINARY reasons, only for POSITIVE REINFORCEMENT. I handle problems "in house," where I can control any necessary logical consequences.

I make a pledge that if they follow our basic school and classroom rules, and should ever be wrongfully blamed, accused, get into trouble for something they didn't do, I WILL DEFEND THEM AGAINST ANYONE, another teacher, principal, ANY adult or child, as long as they are telling me the truth and the whole story. Should they not tell me the truth, it will take some time before I can trust them again.

We don't spend a lot of time on academics the first day as it takes all of us a while to get back into a routine. I give them informal, non-threatening assessments, disguised as "review," in each of the basic subjects. I pass out a math assessment, and let them know that "This is not a test, I just want to see what you remember. If you know this stuff already, I don't want to bore you."

"Until we get your photos, we need pictures of you so visitors know who's in our class. I would like you to draw a picture of yourself and sign it at the bottom of the page since you're the artist. You may use crayons, colored pencils, markers, or you may choose to make a pencil sketch." *"Can we draw just the head? Can we spike our hair, add a mustache, pierce our ears, nose, eyebrows...?"* "Draw yourself so someone who knows you will recognize you."

I am able to discern so much from their artwork, their developmental level, self-image, drawing ability. It never ceases to amaze me how one can recognize these kids from the personalities present in their self-portraits.

I have a motivational poem on the board near the door where the children enter and exit, so it is the first and last thing that they see every day. I have written it out on strips so that I can adjust the spacing to allow for their photos. As soon as the kids seem comfortable with me and can relax for the sitting, I bring my old-school SLR camera with portrait lens. Yes, "selfies" are also accepted, whatever makes them happy. I like to cut the 4 x 6 print down to 4 x 4 and frame the image on a deckled (torn edge) 5 x 5 piece of black paper because later I have other uses for them.

YOU ARE A MARVEL
by Pablo Casals

Do you know what you are? You are a marvel.
You are unique.
In all the years that have passed there has never
    been another child like you.
The way you move, *the way you think,*
    your gifts and talents,
    the way you view the world
Your legs, your arms, your clever fingers,
You have the capacity for anything.

    Yes, you are a marvel. Can you then harm
        another, who is, like you, a marvel?

    (I added the thoughts in italics, which I'm pretty sure Pablo would approve.)

We spend a few minutes discussing the meaning of the poem, the definition of the word **marvel**, what a miracle each of them is, how there has never been another person on the planet like them, how special each and every one of us is.

I sneak in a little science and math, the fact that we breathe without any effort or thought, for as long as about 100 years, that our heart continues to beat about 70 times every minute for the rest of our lives. I show them the math... 70 x 60 = 4,200 beats per hour   24 x 4,200 = 100,800 beats per day... x 365... x 100

You may prefer a thought like, YOU ARE MORE ___ (AMAZING, AWESOME...) THAN YOU CAN EVER IMAGINE. BE YOURSELF!

I tell them, and reinforce throughout the year, that they are not better than anyone else, and that
NOBODY, NO MATTER THEIR TITLE, POSITION, OR AMOUNT OF MONEY THEY POSSESS, IS BETTER THAN THEM!

Time to squeeze in a bit of reading. I usually use an older (whole language) book which has good literature, and is not our current adoption, to get an idea of their reading abilities. I begin with volunteers, until the others become more comfortable. If they are reluctant readers, I don't force them but make a note to listen to them read individually later.

Switching back and forth between academics and non-academics the first day back will help ease them (and you) into the regimen, so I might next discuss our ARTIST OF THE MONTH board, a method I employ to introduce my students to art, artists, different mediums and styles.

To test for phonemic awareness, auditory discrimination, and spelling skills, I give a quick spelling inventory which includes all of the short and long vowels, and allows me to screen for other challenges.

I try to get a writing sample from each child. Depending on time, it might be an entry in our journals, or possibly a short essay on what they would like to do this year. Besides reading and math, what other fun things would you like to learn in ___ grade? Or, you can always fall back on the old standard, "What I Did On My Summer Vacation."

If you don't get everything you planned accomplished the first day, no problem, there's always tomorrow.

"Everything changed the day he (she) figured out that there was exactly enough time for the important things in his (her) life." —Brian Andreas

MY BAD
(Or A Few Of The Many Times I Blew It)

Here is concrete proof that you won't be the first, and certainly won't be the last, to make a mistake:

Early in my career, I "inherited" a student who already had two strikes and was being given one last chance before he was expelled. I don't remember what he had done but he didn't seem all that difficult, I mean he was a second grader! Since this was during my "barely surviving" stage, I didn't possess a bag of tricks to work with. L.J., a child who was well-liked and looked up to by the others, possibly a bit feared, assumed the job of class sergeant-at-arms, and became my "right-hand man."

One morning in the middle of oral reading we all heard someone say something that shouldn't have been said in any classroom. Our eyes popped, my eyebrows must have reached my hairline (which wasn't that high at the time). I looked to L.J. and he shook his head in the affirmative. *"Yes, he actually said that, Mr. Anderson!"* I questioned the class with my eyes. Though horrified, they managed to convey to me, *"Yes, he did!"*

Then it just came out. "All right, that's it! Do you want it **WITH YOUR PANTS ON** OR **YOUR PANTS OFF**?" I blurted. *"IN FRONT OF THE GIRLS?"* the entire class questioned in classic primary student unison. Yes, I actually said that!

The student must have believed that I would actually do this (This was during the era when corporal punishment was sanctioned, although not something I would ever consider), because we never had even a tiny problem for the rest of the year! If it was ever repeated to anyone else outside the classroom, I never heard about it.

Around that same time, I found out that I would have a boy in my class who in kindergarten and first grade was sent home or suspended almost every day, and for most of first grade he had been put on half days. I quickly did my research and found that he had an older cousin with whom I was acquainted. On the first day of class I brought up this fact with the child, and told him that I'd be speaking to his cousin each week, and telling him about all the *good* things that he (my student) was doing in class. For whatever reason (I think his "problem" was more a lack of respect for women), everything went well most of the year until, in response to one of my questions, he proclaimed, *"This conversation is over!"* Rather than stopping, taking a breath, maybe counting to ten, I made the HUGE MISTAKE of saying, "You're right, this conversation **has** ended. You're going to see the principal!"

Understand that this was a kid who had been great for the majority of the year. He had improved over the previous year in leaps and bounds, and then made one mistake! I really overreacted! My intention of a short talk with the principal before he returned to class, became a five day suspension! While in the principal's office, he first kicked her and then punched the vice-principal who had arrived to provide assistance.

So, rather than remembering those 175 days of second grade as a time of remarkable progress, both academically and socially, he undoubtedly recalls the time that he was suspended for a week! I am not that fond of this term, but... MY BAD!

This was the day that I pledged to take care of behavior problems on my own, and to visit the principal's office only when we were celebrating the positive.

Another early faux pas was the time I inverted a child (yes, upside down) over the garbage can. He HAD been fooling around, which didn't excuse my childish behavior, after all I *was* a couple decades older.

I recall using the word STUPID only once or twice, but it did surface in a discussion we were having about name calling. I remember opining that whomever started the saying, "Sticks and stones may break my bones, but words (names) will never hurt me," was STUPID! I went on to say that "Words can be just as painful as broken bones, that broken bones usually heal while words and names can scar someone for life!"

Most of the class were shaking their heads like they understood, and agreed with what I was saying, except for one girl who had her head down and was crying. Soon she lifted her head and declared, *"My grandmother is not stupid!"* "Of course she isn't, what she was telling you was that___, and she was right!" Oh, well, tomorrow's a new day!

When I gave a writing assignment I would usually give the children specific parameters, including the required length of the exercise. Other times I would leave it open-ended and explain that they should write just enough to tell us what they wanted us to know, and that one person might be able to do this in two pages while another might find it necessary to write five. One child continued to ask, "But how long should **mine** be, how long should **mine** be?" Perhaps it had been a particularly stressful day because I admit to saying, "seventeen pages!" The next day I received a note (I still have it) which stated that ___ could not do seventeen pages, she could only do three. I was chastised, learned a lesson, and apologized to the child and the parent, for whom English was his second language.

Kids know if you care about them, and if you do, they are loyal and forgiving.

7 THE "OTHER" BASICS

SELF-ESTEEM

Essential to one's well-being, is their self-esteem, their self-worth. Good self-esteem can make the difference between a happy, well-lived life and one that is fraught with sadness and insecurities.

Psychologists, psychiatrists, therapists, tell us that because of "something" in one's childhood that has happened/not happened, been said/not said, without the appropriate interventions, a person may struggle with this "issue" for the rest of their lives.

This "something" could be a death, illness, alcohol or substance abuse in the family, verbal or physical abuse, not living up to a parent's (or other trusted person's) expectations, not being protected by a parent, sometimes being in the foster care system, poverty… At the risk of sounding like a DYLAN lyric, if one has been neglected, dejected, rejected or not protected, subjected, suspected, inspected or misdirected, dissected, expected, selected or overly corrected… one could be a candidate for some guidance and support. Because of this "something," a person might become a bully, join a gang, commit a crime, have a history of bad relationships, be depressed, suicidal, have alcohol or substance abuse problems, food insecurities… You can surely add to this list.

It is my belief that one's self-esteem can be FOSTERED, BOLSTERED, REJUVENATED, AND MAINTAINED, relatively easily, IF IT IS DONE AT AN EARLY AGE.

This will be a common thread throughout the fabric of this book, and I will be making suggestions, and offering ideas which have worked with some of my students. The transformation that one sees in a child who has gained a bit of confidence, increased their self-worth, is mind-boggling, and well worth the extra effort. I understand that this is a very complex issue, and that some of my examples, approaches, and results may seem over-simplified.

Many, including some educators, are convinced that self-esteem is not that big a deal, or that it will come eventually, once the child has learned "what they're supposed to." What about those who never master the required skills, the 10 or 20 percent who struggle with reading, writing, or math? Where and when are they expected to acquire their self-worth? What about those who are doing well academically but lack confidence, security?

Every child should know that THEY ALREADY HAVE YOUR "SEAL OF APPROVAL," that THEY HAVE VALUE FOR WHO THEY ARE RIGHT NOW.

COMMUNICATION

To say that we have a communication problem today is a gross understatement. To begin with we have a chronic LISTENING PROBLEM. Many don't possess the listening skills to carry on a meaningful conversation. Even if one has shared values, and cares deeply for another, a conversation and relationship can suffer if one is not aware of and able to understand the other person's communication style.

Our country is now divided very nearly right down the middle. We tend to congregate with those who think like we do, and often conclude that the other half is not worth listening to. Regard our so-called "representatives" in Congress. Rather than searching for common ground, oaths are taken to dismiss, ignore, the ideas, opinions, and suggestions of the "opposition." Compromise is a dirty word.

The face-to-face communication we once enjoyed at family gatherings, lunches with friends, are often undermined because some fear that they may miss something if they don't keep current on the electronic device which they are covertly monitoring. The individuals we once greeted on our neighborhood walks are often so addicted to their device of choice that they are oblivious to external stimuli.

Competing with "screens" has been a challenge for decades. Hopefully children (and adults) will learn to strike a balance. If they are not capable of meaningful face-to-face communication, including listening to others, personal relationships, not to mention our dealings with the rest of the world, will suffer.

At the very least we need to MODEL good listening and communication skills for our students.

RESPONSIBILITY

Children must be told, shown, trained how to be responsible. There are plenty of ways which we can facilitate this as teachers. One utilized by many teachers is to assign appropriate jobs, tasks, and chores. Kids, all of us, want to feel needed, and that we are contributing. In the early grades, this can be accomplished with monitors and a monitors chart which rotates weekly. Our classroom benefitted from the following help: an attendance taker, one who collected papers and other assignments, one who maintained and kept track of sports equipment, a team who straightened/dusted designated areas such as bookcases, games, counters... Most don't mind the occasional housekeeping chore, especially if everyone is working together, for a short period of time, and they're not getting criticized for their efforts. The most popular jobs were usually those where they could leave the room, emptying the trash, or the favorite of most, being the messenger. This was not only a break from the classroom tedium but a chance to feel special, being trusted to visit the secretary, principal, or another classroom, especially if this is a former teacher, or if one's friends or siblings are in the class.

I expect the students to be responsible for keeping their desks (relatively) neat and organized. I am also a big fan of a school-wide plan for "helping" the custodian or plant manager keep the playground clean. A different grade each week could "police" (the kids love that term) the playground and field for detritus, litter, lost papers and forgotten coats, gloves, and other clothing items.

You might want to help the children understand that what they SAY and DO (and what they DON'T SAY and DO) sometimes has fallout and consequences. They should take into account how their words and actions will affect others.

Children have no trouble understanding why we need laws, although this may be getting harder for them to comprehend as more and more adults, their role models, aren't able to accept that laws are meant for everyone. For starters, maybe the kids can propose and produce a campaign which reminds adults that STOP means what it says, not slow or speed, and that we **stop** at stop signs, that it is a law for a good reason. They could likewise point out to the person in the driver's seat where the turn indicator is located, its purpose, and the reason for the law that states that it must be used. While they're at it, the children could emphasize to the adults that driving is a serious matter, that this is the REAL WORLD not a video game, and that as much as they'd like to be, they are not competing on the NASCAR circuit. Stress to the driver that their child, other passengers, the humans in the other cars, and pedestrians, are MORTAL, they don't come back from the dead like when you reboot your electronic device, and that they need to put away any distracting items and WATCH THE ROAD.

I'd like to revive an "unwritten law" from the not too distant past, one which we took as an "unofficial rule" growing up, one which worked well but has apparently fallen out of fashion. "KEEP TO THE RIGHT" was ingrained in us from a young age. It was uncomplicated and made sense. Unlike the inevitable confusion we now encounter when we approach another pedestrian on the sidewalk, or the turmoil we experience at a congested grocery store, we knew to always move, in single file, to the right. Why do we so often have a problem holding on to the good stuff that works in our society, in our education system?

Guess my old-school expectations have been exposed. Each time I would leave the house as a child (through high-school), I would hear my mother's words before I could sneak out the door. "LET YOUR CONSCIENCE BE YOUR GUIDE" (as spoken to Pinocchio by the Blue Fairy) or "TO THINE OWN SELF BE TRUE" (Polonius speaking to his son in Hamlet, Shakespeare). Whether it was the guilt trip, or knowing that someone cared for you so much that you wouldn't do anything to hurt them, I (usually) did the right thing, well more often than not, so I guess it worked!

SERVICE TO THE COMMUNITY

There are numerous benefits of community service. There are the good feelings that one experiences when helping another person, improved social and cooperative skills, the pride that one feels when they are giving back while helping meet the needs of their community. The children learn to be more respectful of others, more responsible, while they gain the practical training to be the citizens and leaders of tomorrow. They also become more appreciated by the community and are seen as productive members of society, not as problems or burdens. Their elevated confidence and self-esteem will help ensure lower levels of problem behavior.

There was a tradition at one of my schools that on May 1 the primary (K-3) students would divide up the neighborhood and deliver "May baskets," which would contain flowers from the yards of our children's families. The students felt good that they were doing something for others, and were awed by the smiles and happiness tears which their unexpected gifts brought to the recipients. Some of the beneficiaries would drop by the school or write a letter to voice their appreciation for our thoughtfulness.

One such person I have not forgotten was an older woman (older than me) who was leaving her home as we were arriving. She later hunted us down and visited our classroom. It seems that she had been on her way to the hospital for major surgery, and this perfectly-timed appearance, the children's smiles, and her favorite flowers, made her feel that everything would be all right.

The intermediate students (4-6) could do something similar for the neighborhood, possibly bringing rakes on a designated day in the fall, to gather and remove the leaves for those who were incapable.

Another excellent lesson for children is a visit to a "senior citizen" or convalescent home. This can be a bit scary initially for the kids (and often for the teachers), but soon most feel comfortable, presenting a personal card, a piece of art to be displayed on the wall, reciting their poems, singing a group song, or just talking to the residents. These trips are always full of unplanned adventures, and it is beneficial to prepare the children for what to expect and some possible "surprises." The holiday seasons are always popular, so visits at other times of the year are especially appreciated. We have been surprised on occasion with warm, straight-out-of-the-oven baked goods from the seniors.

Yet another opportunity for the children to learn empathy, thinking about others, is writing to the troops who are serving overseas. A simple hand-made card, addressed to a soldier, telling them a bit about yourself, letting them know that you are thinking about them and appreciate what they are doing for our country. Explain to the kids that this is not the appropriate time to voice anti-war or political sentiments. The responses that we received, the cards, letters, and patches, not only brought long-lasting smiles, great pride, and puddles of accumulated tears, but were a reminder of the difference one can make with a few heart-felt lines, in this case to a person who is longing to get back home to a country that many of us take for granted. The Marines stationed in the Middle East assured us that the child-made cards that we sent, along with our letters, were displayed on the walls of the rec room and had been read and re-read multiple times by all. The snowflakes, they informed us, would be the closest thing that they would see to snow until they returned to "the states" as the temperatures were "well into the 100s there." This simple gesture brought much cheer to the servicemen and women, and made them feel appreciated.

How about a project which will help the environment, as well as provide you with a science unit, and a little art thrown in? Each year we would help the Department of Forestry grow oak saplings from acorns, and take a voluntary field trip to plant them in a designated area. We would kick-off the unit by brainstorming a list of things that we get from a tree (What A Tree Has Done For Us Lately). Give a short art lesson on drawing a basic tree (without leaves), sketching it with a pencil and then outlining it with a dark crayon or marker. Lay a piece of 8 ½ x 11 copy paper over the drawing, and secure it with a couple paper clips. Following the outline of the trunk, branches, possibly a knot hole, maybe some grass, write as many of the words from the class-generated list as will fill up all of the lines. Repeat the words if necessary. When you are finished, you will have a tree comprised of words. Cut around the shape of the tree (bare or with leaves), adhere this to a green piece of construction paper, possibly frame them in blue, and display them on a bulletin board during the time you are growing the saplings.

Maybe help the Department of Fish and Game raise salmon (or another fish), releasing them into the river when they get to the fry stage, to continue their journey. Of course, this will be accompanied by a science lesson, and in our case, a field trip to a nearby fish hatchery where we also learned a bit about life and death.

CAUSE AND EFFECT

A friend and colleague of mine teaches her kindergarteners the basics of cause and effect. She uses an example that many of her students can relate to: If you hit someone (cause), they will probably get angry (effect), and may try to hit you back, possibly harder. If one is smaller or less powerful they might strike back in an unexpected way. She is assured that most of her five-year olds understand, even if many of the rest of us don't.

It never fails that if my neighbor doesn't rake her leaves, and clear out the gutters (cause), when the predicted storm arrives we wake up to a clogged drain and a flooded intersection (effect).

On the evening news, we learn that a bridge has collapsed (the effect), or we drive down a local street dodging potholes, and we hear from our mechanic that our tires are wearing improperly, that we need a wheel alignment (the effects). What precipitated these calamities, these hazardous conditions, these unexpected costs? Could it have something to do with failing to maintain our infrastructure (the cause)?

8   DISCIPLINE

With few exceptions, MOST young children want structure and parameters because they don't enjoy being in a classroom which lacks order and organization. Kids want to be in a safe, comfortable environment where they can learn. If you are respectful, fair, and reasonable, they want you to be in charge.

When I was new to teaching, I made a point of scrutinizing other teachers' discipline plans since I didn't yet have one to call my own. Those which seemed to work the best were those one didn't notice. The ones which were more obvious didn't always impress me. There was the "upper-grade" teacher who carried around a baseball bat and scowled, or another who seemed to have an endless supply of full-length movies. On the first day of school, one teacher would, without warning, slam down a yardstick, hard enough to break it, startling the students (and me). This annual ritual (and sacrifice) was designed to act as a deterrent to misbehavior, to put fear in their hearts. I often observed one red-faced educator screaming at his kids, "I MEAN IT THIS TIME! I'M GOING TO COUNT TO THREE... ONE, TWO..." as they literally ran around, and out of the room. A former nun would find solace, peace, oblivion, in the corner of the room, where she would go to pray when things got rough.

Especially if you are new to the profession, your rules should be planned and written down when the children arrive on the first day of school. Keep it simple, with no more than four or five rules for the younger ones. They could be something like:

Raise your hand when you want to speak.
Use your inside voice.
Keep your hands and feet to yourself.
Follow directions the first time they are given.

Discuss why rules are necessary, so kids can learn, and so there isn't utter confusion and disorder in the classroom. Continue to review these rules and others which are not written down but must be followed. Kids will observe you for a while, so don't be over-confident if the first day or week goes remarkably well. This is often the honeymoon period. Within a week or two, they will have figured you out, determined any weaknesses, and might begin to test you. Do you really mean what you say? If you are big on fairness (like I was), you might begin to hear, "That's not fair!"

From day one, BE CONSISTENT. If you're not, they will make your day and your life miserable. Err on being (a little) too strict rather than being a wimp. One can always loosen up a bit, it's harder to go the other way.

Choose the all-important discipline plan with care, selecting one which will be fair, simple to manage, complement your personality, and accomplish what it was meant to do. Some elect to use the age-old system where right off the bat, bam, zero tolerance, at the slightest infraction, your name is written on the board. Subsequent offenses are documented with a check mark. Then there are some so-called positive discipline plans which are similar to the aforementioned plan with the addition of the "positive" statements made before one's name is recorded for all to see. As children enter the room, the teacher might announce to the class, "I like the way ___ is coming in quietly," or "I like the way ___ is getting right to work." Then it's open season on anyone who is not following the example of those you have complimented, anyone is fair game.

Then there's the popular "card system." This method usually involves a system of colored cards, either kept in the child's desk or on a bulletin board, "the wall of guilt." After each infraction, another card is turned over or removed, with a designated consequence, for instance, the first one might be a warning, or a missed recess. The second, a missed recess and a call home, the third, a trip to the principal's office. I personally don't care for these types of plan as they are based on fear and threats, can be abused, and once a child has his/her card turned over or taken away, they often give up. You've proven to them what they already knew, that they are BAD. It is easier for them to face the consequences than to try to live up to the high expectations. That said, it might be a good option for a new teacher, or one who is not yet secure with their "control."

Some choose plans incorporating peer pressure, dropping marbles into a small, transparent jar, or row (group) points. When the jar is full, or the group has earned a certain number of points, there might be a popcorn party, extra recess, or some other reward. Another involves adding a letter on the board, whenever the group is displaying the hoped-for behavior, with the goal to spell out a phrase, for instance ICE CREAM PARTY. I have utilized all of these fairly successfully, and they have accomplished my short-term goal, until the novelty wears off.

I prefer a more positive plan, one based on mutual respect, where the children want to do the responsible thing because it's the right thing to do. We respect each other, trust each other, and are working towards a common goal which benefits all of us.

Make sure that the consequences which you adopt are logical, and relate to the infraction.

Equally important to the equanimity of the classroom, is that the children understand your PROCEDURES (as they vary from teacher to teacher), what you expect, how you want things done. This might encompass what you should do when you enter the room, your pencil breaks, you finish your work, you have a question or problem, or the bell rings. Model the conduct that you expect, and check for understanding.

Come up with a signal or saying to employ when you want the kids to stop their work and give you their full attention. Some which have worked for me are: clapping out a rhythm, to which the kids respond by mimicking the pattern, finger cymbals, a pleasant-sounding bell, or a rain stick, a chord played on a keyboard or autoharp, or F-R-E-E-Z-E, P-L-E-A-S-E. Others use 1, 2, 3, EYES ON ME, to which the kids respond, 1, 2, EYES ON YOU. Whatever works.

TWEAKING

If you decide that the relatively minor action, behavior of a child warrants some tweaking, perhaps an attitude adjustment, make every effort to preserve their dignity, the foundations of their personality. Aspire to achieve this without breaking their spirit.

THE LOOK

An integral component to my discipline approach is a kind of stare/glare which I have cultivated and honed over the years, which I utilize infrequently when a child has broken a sacred rule, violated an unspoken law, or committed a transgression. It incorporates a combination of feigned shock, disbelief, and a small dose of guilt-tripping in conjunction with slightly raised eyebrows. The kids begin practicing "THE LOOK" early in the year, and soon master its intricacies. I pretend to chastise them for their lack of seriousness, and they laugh, unless "THE LOOK" is directed at them. Just ask Noah.

Noah was having a wonderful time shoving crayons into our heavy-duty electric pencil sharpener, until he discovered that the colored wax was melting, thus plugging the workings and rendering the machine unusable. To his credit, he soon reported what he had done and apologized profusely.

"What do you think the logical consequences should be, Noah, when you have damaged someone else's property?" "*I guess I should have to replace it,*" he responded. "Well, here's the name of the manufacturer and the model number. You may use the computer to look it up." Shortly, we heard the loud groaning and moaning, due to the $175.00 price tag! "Do you want to talk to your mom first, or do you want me to call her?" "*I'll tell her,*" *he answered.* Later that day, before I left the school, Noah's mom walked into the room, embarrassed. "*I just talked with Noah,*" she said, attempting to smile. *"He told me what happened, and I asked him, 'Mr. A must have been mad, did he yell at you?'* "OH NO, MUCH WORSE," *Noah responded gravely,* "HE GAVE ME THE LOOK!"

I told her that I had already found someone to repair the sharpener, that he would have to take it apart and boil it out. If it was amenable to her, we would charge Noah a nominal fee so that he would remember this experience, and hopefully not repeat it. Upon hearing the amount, Noah was quite relieved.

REWARDS

Rewards in my class were not (usually) candy, small prizes, or as in some well-funded private schools, new athletic shoes or a trip to a far-off country. A cherished dividend for hard work, reaching a goal, or another accomplishment, was a chance to work in a kindergarten class or to team with a "special needs" child.

As adults, we are aware of the intangible benefits one receives from helping another. When a first, second, or third-grader is assisting a younger child, they become an instant celebrity. To a five-year old, any older child is a SUPER-HERO! Imagine what that can do for a child lacking in confidence and self-esteem!

A win-win situation for all involved. A young child better understands a concept (Children are often the best teachers), while an older child learns what it means, feels like, to be needed, appreciated. One teacher gains an aide, and another has a student who now feels better about themselves, and will hopefully work harder and be more successful in class.

We show our thanks, our appreciation for this symbiotic, mutually-beneficial relationship, by including these children when we fly our kites, shoot off our rockets, or any activity which we feel they might enjoy.

That said, when you are starting out, if necessary for survival, go ahead and BRIBE the kids. It will work for a while until you have a chance to get it together.

CONFLICT RESOLUTION

Ideally, kids (and the rest of us) would be able to resolve most conflicts on their own, without the help of adults or another child. When this is not possible, when intervention is necessary, you might want to utilize the following strategy.

Rules of Engagement

If possible, this exchange takes place on a bench, just outside the classroom, where I can observe the proceedings.

Flip a coin, or call rock, paper, scissors, to determine who goes first. Clear your mind of all extraneous thoughts, those which have nothing to do with the situation at hand.

Look at the other person, concentrate on them, (really) listen to what they are saying without interrupting.

Repeat the gist of what they said. Do you agree, have any problems with their depiction of what happened, has been happening?

The other person then has the floor, and the same rules apply.

A discussion follows, with a facilitator looking on. The participants attempt to resolve the issue by themselves. Does this discussion need to involve anyone else? Does either party deserve a consequence? Are we all in agreement with the solution, and clear where we go from here?

Periodically revisit, discuss, and role-play the Rules of Engagement in class throughout the year.

I handle escalated disputes differently than some. If two children are having long-standing difficulties getting along, I was taught to have them say "sorry," keep them apart, make them promise that they will not get anywhere near each other for the rest of their lives. In contrast to this advice, I have them spend (at least) the lunch recess together.

We might hear moans and groans, and mumbles of "No way!" I tell them that I hope we can settle this problem among the three of us, and not have to bring in their parents or the principal. They usually change their tune.

The two talk, informing each other about their family, their likes, dislikes, and hobbies. When they return to the classroom after lunch, I find time to meet with them, outside if possible. Each child tells me three or four things that they learned about the other. "Did you find anything that you have in common, any ways that you are alike? Is there anything that you might be able to help ___ with? How about you, is there anything that you can help ___ with?" More often than not, this is able to assuage the strife.

9 FRIENDSHIP

Everybody needs friends, at least one. Children need assistance understanding the complex, often mysterious, sometimes hurtful aspects of friendship. They need to be told (by a trusted person) what to look for in a friend, and that to have a good friend one must be a good friend. Kids are able to come up with the desirable traits which a friend should have: honesty, loyalty, one who respects you for who you are inside (not because you're rich or popular), one that you can have fun with, one who brings out the best in you. It helps if you have some common interests but if not, friends can share and learn new skills together and bring out hidden interests and talents.

One doesn't have to be friends with everyone, but they should be civil with all. Best friends will sometimes hurt each other and have a falling out. They know each other very well, and know exactly how to get under the other's skin. It's all right to take a time-out, a break, from a friendship. It may resume after this period, or if it doesn't work out, as much as it doesn't seem possible at the time, there are other people out there who would be delighted to be their friend.

> *"Dear Mr. A, Thank you for listening to my problems and helping me through rough times. Things got better, you were right! I did what you said, I called her and talked to her.*
>
> *Thanks again. P.S. You gave me the best advice I had ever heard of."*
>
> —A former student, who was in sixth-grade at the time of this letter.

It's healthy to have more than one friend, but to keep them one must continue to treat them all with respect. If a "friend" wants to "own" you, wants you to forget all others, is maybe "mean" to your other friends (or you), you should question their motives and reconsider their friendship.

You may want to follow up later with a kind of self-assessment. In addition to revisiting the beneficial traits, consider these questions: Are they continuing to be a good friend? To how many of these can they check "Yes?" Am I a good listener, or do I do all of the talking? Am I aware of my friend's feelings? Do I sometimes try to see things from their point of view? Am I honest with them about how I feel, what I believe, or do I tell them what I think they want to hear?

It's vital that the children understand that EVERYONE at times FEELS ALONE, even SAD. It's crucial that they know that they have a BFF (Best Friend Forever) with them at all times…THEMSELVES! They need to know, You are a good, interesting person, and can be your own best friend.

"I wish I could show you when you are lonely or in darkness the astounding light of your own being."
—14th century poet Hafiz

Primary teachers often have their kids make a "Book About Me." This might consist of their name, members of their family, pets, and could also include: I am good at _____ , and _____. The things I like about myself are ___. My friends are___. I am happy when ___, and I am sad when ___. Their answers are often revealing, and should be read carefully and taken seriously.

Early in the year, and periodically, check to be sure that EVERY child has a friend. Make every effort to find a good match for those who don't.

"I can still remember the day (as a seven-year old) I met ___ , and having a conversation with you about how helping someone else

out helps you feel better about yourself. That's something that I still regularly think about, and try to live by, to this day. So, thanks."

—A former student, who maintains his twenty-year friendship with this second-grade classmate.

10 POSITIVE THINKING
A Successful Year

One of the first homework assignments I give in the year is called ABCs For A Successful Year. This is intended as a collaborative project for the student and their entire family, one which will start everyone off on the right track, with a good attitude. It is also meant to encourage communication between the child, their parents and other family members.

Using the letters of the alphabet (in alphabetical order), come up with 26 ideas to make this a more positive, successful school year for you and your child. The key word should begin with that letter, and may be located anywhere in the sentence. For example:

- A **Always** do your best.
- B Get up **bright** and early.
- C Make it a point to be **courteous**.

BE CREATIVE, AND HAVE FUN!

"I'M SPECIAL" BOOK

At Back-To-School Night, I provide the family representatives with six pieces of 7" x 9" colored paper, and a sheet of instructions. Their assignment is to distribute these to the parents, grand-parents, aunts, uncles, and siblings of the child, my student. Each person will write the nicest note that they can, mentioning all of the many (sincere) reasons why the child is APPRECIATED, RESPECTED, AND LOVED. They should incorporate WORDS OF ENCOURAGEMENT and SUPPORT, maybe awaken fond memories of an event or story which might elicit a smile or laugh. Return them in the envelope addressed to me, impressing on the child that these are to be delivered UNOPENED.

At school, we construct books from paper lunch bags. Cut off the bottom of three bags, lay the bags on top of one another, fold them in half (lengthwise), square off the (unfolded) ends with scissors or a paper cutter. Punch three holes near the folded end of the bags, and using yarn (novelty yarn is fun), shoelaces, jute, whatever works, tie a knot or bow for each of the three holes. Voila, a book with pockets.

If the notes haven't been received after you've reminded the parents, you will want others to write notes, former teachers, you, the principal, classmates, friends, so no one is left out. It is important to screen them before passing them out to make sure that no one has said hurtful things.

Explain that this is just a sampling (a few) of all the people who LOVE THEM, THINK THE WORLD OF THEM, KNOW HOW SPECIAL THEY ARE. Explain, discuss, that all of us get down occasionally, and if that time should come (or when they have a couple minutes of free time) they may take out their "I'M SPECIAL" book, and be reminded of just how awesome they are!

Let the kids decorate the cover and the pages any way they wish, with markers, stickers, crayons, or they may leave it plain.

Allot enough time for them to read a letter or two before they are asked to insert the folded pages into the pockets. The books can be housed in their desks where they will always be available to them. Remind the children that these are CONFIDENTIAL, and that only those people whom they choose will be allowed to see them.

I BE-LEAF IN MYSELF

Early in the fall, before the leaves change colors and start to fall, we do this self-image art project. I ask the kids to bring in a leaf, a fairly large one, or maybe a group of three or five small ones. Supplies needed are a piece of glass, a brayer, water-based ink (I use Speedball black), and white construction paper.

Depending on the age of the child, they or I squeeze the ink onto the glass. Using the brayer, spread out the ink until a thin layer is achieved. Roll the ink onto one side of the leaf (which has been placed on a paper towel) making sure that all of the "veins" are covered. Carefully peel off the leaf and place it ink side down on the construction paper. Cover the leaf with a piece of clean butcher paper, paper towel or scrap paper. While you hold the paper down, the child rubs (I suggest using the pointing, middle, and ring fingers) so that the ink on the leaf transfers to the white paper. With younger kids, I might go over it myself to make sure that no part of the leaf has been missed. Lift off the cover paper and the leaf and you have a print worthy of framing in fall colors, black, whatever you prefer.

The next morning, upon entering the room, the children rush to the bulletin board to examine their print. When they've had ample time to peruse the prints, and while they're still beaming with pride, I have them raise their right hands. "Repeat after me," I tell them, "I PROMISE TO BE-LEAF IN MYSELF!" We can forgive ourselves for all of the little mistakes we've made in our lives thus far, and from this point on we can be the person we choose to be!"

THE FRAME

When one of my students put their heart and soul into a piece of art, a piece of creative writing, a math paper or handwriting practice, I would find myself saying, "Wow, you need to ask your parents to frame that!" At a garage sale, I would discover a faux antique, "gilded," semi-ornate, oval frame which would be perfect for our classroom needs.

I hung the frame just to the right of our door where all the children would see it as the they stood in line or exited the room. At these times, we would talk about what had been posted. Initially, we used the frame to display the multiplication math facts (cards) that many kids were finding difficult to memorize (8 x 7, 6 x 8, the "usual suspects"). Seeing and reciting them for a couple days, most kids would have them emblazoned on their minds and readily retrievable.

The frame would be utilized whenever I wanted them to be aware of or remember something important. It might be a small poster advertising something that was going on at the school or a program on television that I thought they might enjoy or could benefit them.

Then there was the reason I had originally intended it for, that every single child would be represented periodically, with a sample of their creative writing, a piece of artwork, an impressive math paper, or the most perfect cursive "s" ever.

It was, for some of the children, their favorite square foot of wall space in the classroom. It was certainly one of the best investments I ever made for educating kids, and a great vehicle for boosting their self-esteem!

CAUGHT YOU!

A "CAUGHT YOU (BEING GOOD)" board is a way to, right off the bat, show the kids, model for them some of the traits that you think are important. You might start the ball rolling by mentioning that you witnessed so-and-so helping out a classmate or picking up a piece of trash on the playground. Write this observation on a post-it note or card and attach it to a wall, easel, or white board. Make the materials and writing implements available, the cards, notes, markers, push pins, whatever is necessary, so that the children, you, or a visitor can jot down what they saw that impressed them. These commendations should be read and discussed periodically to achieve the hoped-for effect.

Initially, you will be amazed at the number of laudable acts, good deeds that they observe, how clean the playground is, but gradually, what they notice, what they report, will be more realistic. Ideally, these gestures, the kindness, thoughtfulness, helpfulness, concern for others, responsibility, and empathy, will become ingrained, second-nature. You might want to suggest a school-wide board, located in an accessible area, which will benefit all of the children, and possibly improve the behavior and attitude of the entire school population.

PERSONALIZED PLATES

A fun way to learn more about your students, what's lurking in those brains, is to challenge them to design their own personalized license plates. Use one of your own license plates for a pattern. Children may use any (available) color construction paper for the background, and the letters. Stencils or the letters which you use for bulletin boards work well for tracing the letters and numbers. Use markers for writing out the chosen state, motto, and any decorations or illustration. Kids may choose an actual location, a state of mind (happiness, bliss), or an imaginary residence. The message can be (just about) anything which is important to them.

11 LISTENING TO KIDS

I would routinely set aside time to hear the kids' concerns. If I noticed that they were unsettled or agitated, I would bring what we were doing to a close and listen. If we listen to children, we are aware that probably their number one complaint is that they are not listened to. I empathize and sympathize with them.

Many of my colleagues feel that they can't take the time to do this because there are too many other things to get accomplished, that they'll never finish everything if they did. These listening sessions would usually last only ten or fifteen minutes, with a few exceptions which lasted an hour or so. My feeling is that WE CAN'T AFFORD NOT TO TAKE THE TIME TO LISTEN TO THEM.

When they are able to air their grievances, curb their anxiety, worries, and are comforted, the children will work harder, and will make up the "lost" time. So what if they only do 15 of the same type of math practice problems that day, rather than 30. They can do the other problems for homework if necessary.

One of my students had been coming to school noticeably sad and upset. Before we started our lessons for the day, I asked if anyone had anything which they wanted to discuss. Several kids shared things that had been bothering them, and we discussed possible solutions. Emma then told us her story, a common one for this age group. Her parents were getting a divorce. *"It was all my fault!"* "Oh, Emma!" *"And now they don't like me as much as they did."* "Emma, your parents got a divorce because they were having problems that had nothing to do with you. They decided that these problems could not be resolved, and that they couldn't stay together. They both love you more than you can ever imagine." "*That's what THEY told me!*" she exclaimed. "They love you, and trust you enough to tell you the truth!" "*Really?*" she asked. "REALLY!" I said. "*OH!*" (accompanied by a big smile.) She had heard it from her parents, but it took a short conversation with an outsider to understand that there could be life and love after a divorce.

There is usually a learning curve to being efficient in "reading" children (although some teachers appear to have an innate capacity), becoming attuned, sensitive to the clues, flags, signals that something is bothering them, or that they are keeping something in. A tool that worked for me was to furnish each child with a two-sided laminated disc (kept in their desk) which would inform me of their needs. First thing in the morning and after each recess the students would place this three-inch disc in the upper right corner of their desk. If I saw the "GREEN" side it signaled that the child felt that ALL WAS GOOD. If the "RED" side was exposed, I was alerted that, for some reason, they wanted/needed to speak with me. I would try to connect with them as soon as possible. If I detected a large number, or a sea of red, I would make time at our earliest convenience to have a class discussion.

Consider implementing the following program.

D.E.A.L. (DROP EVERYTHING AND LISTEN)

Many schools have adopted a wonderful, motivational program called D.E.A.R. (Drop Everything and Read), which champions the idea that READING IS A GOOD THING. At a designated time during the day everyone at the school site stops whatever they are doing, pulls out a book or other reading material, and reads for about 15 minutes.

Equally important in my eyes, is a plan which one might call D.E.A.L. (DROP EVERYTHING AND LISTEN). At a scheduled time (I find that it works well first thing in the morning), or whenever there is a need, we drop whatever we are doing and take time to LISTEN TO THE CHILDREN. It is my dream that all teachers will make this deal, this pledge, to their students.

I SEE YOU

When I encounter adults (former children) on my journeys, one of their most common grievances is, "As a child, I felt I was invisible to others."

Were I still in the classroom, I would convey this message to my students early in the year: I **see** you, and am doing my best to **hear** you. If you feel that I am missing something, it is important that you somehow communicate to me what I am not understanding, and that you **persevere** until I do.

SUGGESTION BOX

An easy way to gain access to your students' thoughts is the age-old suggestion box.

Providing the children with an opportunity to write down their concerns, suggestions to improve the classroom, the school, the world, or anything else which they wish to communicate to you, will inform you what's going on in their heads, things they may be afraid to say in front of the whole class or to your face. Read the notes promptly, at least daily, and respond to them in a timely matter so that they will know you are listening to them, and care about what they have to say.

The two girls entered the classroom after morning recess, mumbling, glaring at each other! Both raced straight to the suggestion box, grabbed a pencil and notecard and immediately began writing. Thinking that this looked serious, might be critical, I walked over, and removed the only two cards in the box.

"SO-AND-SO IS LYING!" said the one note. "SO-AND-SO IS LYING!" said the other.

LET THE SUNSHINE IN

One simple, effective way to gain support and earn brownie points from parents while elevating your students' self-esteem and motivation is to send "SUNSHINE NOTES." Once school settles down in the fall, I begin writing (hand-written) notes to the parents of my kids, alerting them (usually a huge, pleasant surprise) that their child has done/is doing something for which they should be commended. It might be helping out another child, being attentive, turning in all their homework, anything POSITIVE. You can find a sincere reason for awarding one to every child in your class, even if it is for having good self-control for the whole morning. You can (almost always) be assured that it will reach home, and the benefits are often immediate… greater appreciation and support from the parents and a more attentive, cooperative child.

Initially, I used a pre-printed 8 ½ x 11 paper which had a smiling sun in the corner. I would quickly color the sun yellow, the rays orange and red, and write the personal letter in purple, blue, and green markers. My comment would be something like:

To the parents of___, We can be ESPECIALLY PROUD of ___ . He /She has ___. Keep up the GOOD WORK.
Sincerely, Mr. Anderson

I would take the child on the rounds with me sometime during that day, visiting those I could count on for supportive remarks, telling them about the remarkable accomplishment that this student had achieved. "You must be proud of yourself!" "That's quite amazing!" "You must be glad that he/she is in your room, Mr. A!" We would sometimes make additions to the signature at the bottom of the note.

I better understood the thrill, the uplifting value of a sunshine note when I was fortunate enough to receive one of my own from a second grader in my class. "A GREAT SUNSHINE NOTE FOR A SUNSHINE PERSON!" it proclaimed. "COOL, YOU DID A GREAT JOB! HAVE A NICE DAY!"

Attached to my note was a redesigned, much happier, warmer sun which I used from then on. To this day, I have kept and continue to cherish this note.

12 CHARACTER EDUCATION

Character education is an organized effort to develop in children the core values, ethics, which are accepted by most people. A program attempts to teach such qualities as respect, responsibility, empathy, honesty, perseverance, and service.

I have been in schools which have spent a great deal of money to purchase materials, lesson plans, scripted books, posters of children portraying the gamut of emotions, the chosen qualities written out in various places in the school, often in multiple languages.

These plans can be an excellent reminder of what should be a part of any good educational program. One can spend thousands of dollars on a character education curriculum, mandate that all of the students read the chapters, discuss all of the pictures, and demand that the desired qualities and their definitions are posted in every classroom and on walls all over the school. These exercises, however, will make little difference, waste a lot of time and money, if these traits are not being modeled by the "ADULTS in the room," the teachers, principal, and other staff members, EVERY SINGLE DAY of the year.

13 DISABILITIES

"Kindness is a language that the deaf can hear and the blind can see."
— Mark Twain

Each year I would invite a person who was blind and another who was deaf (either together or separately) to spend part of the day with us. Occasionally, we had volunteers from the Canine Companions for Independence visit us, along with a working dog or two.

We were taught to "see" through the eyes of a blind person, and were told, shown how they were able to shop, cook, manage their dinner plate, tell time, read, get around independently, with a cane or the help of a guide dog, even play baseball (and beat sighted teams). We tried to experience what it was like being without sight by utilizing blindfolds (strips of cotton sweatshirts) during a (clay) sculpture lesson, a lunch in the classroom, and a (partner) walk around the school… which included tours of the cafeteria, bathrooms, another classroom, and the playground.

We tried to empathize with a deaf person, what they experience, the isolation they sometimes feel living in a world devoid of sound (or the noise which is often so annoying to the rest of us), how difficult it is to learn how to speak for those who have never heard what is audible to most of us. They smiled when I told them about the deaf kids I was working with feeling the vibrations of the reproduction Liberty Bell which they were able to ring, and were happy to discover that we were learning sign language. They laughed when the kids told them of their teacher who would suggest on (noisy) bus field trips that they speak to their neighbors in the expressive (and QUIET) language.

The volunteers from Canine Companions informed us of the possible tasks that a service dog might perform in order to increase the independence of their human. They might turn on/off lights, pull a wheel chair, push buttons, help in a special needs class, a re-habilitation or psychiatric program, act as a "hearing dog," alerting their partner to sounds like doorbells, smoke alarms, alarm clocks, or someone calling their name.

One year we (the entire third-grade class) were fortunate to spend an entire morning with an organization which provides "disability awareness." Our students were able to practice maneuvering wheel chairs, experience mobility canes, touch and manipulate prosthetics, artificial limbs, write in Braille, and learn a bit about what it was like to have a neuro-developmental challenge.

The volunteers shared their insights and personal experiences openly and honestly, and the children gained a greater understanding, sensitivity, and respect for their disabled brothers and sisters. They learned to look beyond a disability, to see a person with similar feelings, needs, and desires as them. They did, one can hope, share this awareness, and attitude, with others.

GABRIELLE

Every so often a child comes along who teaches you far more than you can teach them. Such was the case with Gabrielle. The week before school started, her parents dropped by to introduce themselves and to inform me that Gabrielle would be in my class and that she was in the early stages of Muscular Dystrophy. What do I need to know? What are her physical limitations? Do I need to rearrange the room setting? They advised me to just treat her like I would any of my other students, and that Gabrielle would let me know if there was something that she was unable to do. She was obviously born into the right family.

From the first time I met this confident, serene young girl, I had the sense that she felt comfortable in her own skin. Gabrielle seemed to know more about the important things in life than those who were decades her senior. One got the impression that she was put on this earth to be a model for the rest of us, to inspire us to be better people.

The only times I saw Gabrielle the least bit upset were when she felt that I was considering treating her differently than the other kids, making an exception for her. She would admonish me with this mock scolding look, reminding me that I didn't need to worry about her. Even though Gabrielle had to work harder, physically, than anyone in the class, once she had completed her work she would routinely ask me, "Now, Mr. Anderson, what can I do for you?" It never failed to bring tears to my eyes.

Gabrielle reinforces my consciousness that we should not define others by their differences, disabilities, and other challenges. She is a beautiful, selfless person who happens to have MD. I and anyone fortunate enough to cross paths with Gabrielle will never forget her.

14 BULLYING

No one should be surprised that we have bullying in schools, after all it is prevalent in all other segments of our society. We observe it every day on television, in movies, and in video games. We see it in some of our authority figures, elected "representatives," world leaders, drivers on our streets and highways. We hear bullies on the radio, witness them in the workplace, in all walks of life, even in some classrooms and principals' offices. Social media is the perfect venue to anonymously channel, project our anger, self-hatred, lack of self-worth, onto others.

The kids know who the bullies are, and the young ones will expose them. I am often astonished to hear who they are, but one doesn't have to look far to find the genesis…a parent, boyfriend or girlfriend of the father or mother, a sibling, relative or friend of the family, who has bullied, belittled or teased the child, whittled away at their confidence.

I have attended numerous seminars on bullying, and usually leave disagreeing with much of their reasoning. From my observations, a bully is often one who has been bullied themselves, has possibly been abused verbally or physically. A bully is unable to deal with their anger, and feels powerless to do anything about it. They probably have little self-esteem, and feel that they have no one with whom they can talk (if they aren't in deep denial), or haven't even considered that they could or should.

My first experience with bullying was in the fifth grade. The bully was a friend of mine, who all of a sudden wanted to fight me. My second experience was during this same time, when a boy of middle school age kicked in the fender brace on my bike, and then stole the bag of treats which I was taking to my Cub Scout meeting. My next encounter was not until seventh grade when a classmate would taunt me, and try to pick a fight whenever he saw me. He tried to enlist the services of others, who laughed at him, as most were friends of mine. The bullying escalated until one rainy day when, on the way to an assembly, I bumped him off an elevated walkway into the mud in front of about a hundred kids. I had had ENOUGH! Eventually, he would give up on me and move onto others.

Each case was a horrible experience, and generated a great deal of anxiety. Fortunately, I did not blame myself for any of their actions. I eventually concluded that my default expression, an almost perpetual smile, could have contributed to, provoked, their actions. I theorized that some who were not happy with their situation assumed (wrongly) that, because of this seemingly happy expression, I was devoid of problems.

I tried to understand these unfortunate people. I became aware that my former fifth grade friend was losing his mother to cancer, and that he would be moving back to the country of his birth. I ran into the punk, the thief who had damaged my bike and stole my candy bars, at a football game when I was in high school. I introduced myself, explained who I was, and asked him if he still beat up on younger, smaller children, if he wanted to talk about it. Maybe it was because I was with three of my friends, all of us much taller than he, that he didn't appear interested in continuing the conversation. The third boy I spoke about lost his last fight in this world the night he spit on a stranger. He was no match for the bullet which took his life.

I've since learned that there are many who want others to be as miserable as they are. Fortunately, many children can be taught to ignore these individuals and their issues. Lucas, one of my third-graders, came in from morning recess and asked if he could speak with me. Once we were alone, he said,

"*Mr. Anderson, someone called me a name.*"

"I am so sorry, Lucas. I bet that hurt!"

"Yes, it did!" he said.

I asked, "Don't you feel sorry for him?"

"What? No, Mr. Anderson, he called ME a name."

"Yes, Lucas. Imagine how he must feel inside to say something so hurtful to you! Some people feel so bad about themselves that they have to take it out on others! If they think that what they say bothers you, and if they get away with it, they will continue to do it!"

Lucas smiled and said, *"I GET IT, Mr. Anderson!"*

We would discuss and role-play what one should do and say if they are approached by a bully in a school setting. I explain to them that they might be tempted to say something like, "My big brother is going to beat you up," or "Wow, my teacher, parents, and the principal would be interested in hearing that!" "You might think of punching them. If you are at school, try not to do or say anything, just walk or run away and tell your teacher, another teacher, the principal, or an adult. If the person you tell doesn't do anything, or ignores you, tell another person until someone takes care of the situation to your satisfaction. When you get home, tell your parents the entire story right away."

I was glad that Lucas came directly to me. He is a gentle person, but large and strong enough that he could have solved the problem in a less satisfactory (for the school and the other person), less peaceful way. Lucas would visit our classroom for many years, relating his experience to my current students.

What I said to Lucas worked for him and many others. He understood and trusted that his parents and I would take care of him. I failed to comprehend at the time that this does not work for all kids. There are some children who are so "sensitive" that they feel overly sorry for the bully, and might feel that it was their fault if the bully got in trouble.

Of course, there are those who are going to be afraid to tell because they are worried that the bully will "get even with them," and those who don't want to be labeled a "tattle-tale" or a "baby." Many don't tell because they don't trust adults to do anything about it.

Make sure that the children understand that IT IS NOT THEIR FAULT (unless they were being provocative). IT IS THE BULLY WHO IS TO BLAME, and they should tell someone immediately so that the situation can be taken care of, and the guilty party punished (and helped).

15 GLOSSOPHOBIA

As a child, I experienced a feeling which I couldn't articulate at the time. I felt strongly that I often occupied a parallel plane, not a higher one or lower one, just a different one. It was a comfortable place, and one in which I felt secure. I knew that I was loved, I liked myself, and was confident in my abilities and was not troubled by this state. In class I would complete whatever work was presented to me, raise my hand when a question was posed, and adapt to being ignored. I became adept at entertaining myself. I "floated" through most of elementary school, and it wasn't until seventh or eighth grade when I took geometry that I had a rude awakening, a blow to my stasis. When I was expected, for the first time ever, to speak in front of the classroom (while performing an oral proof), I realized that I was afraid of talking in front of a group, of public speaking, a fear known as glossophobia. I should have recognized this earlier as it was one of the reasons I quit piano lessons as an eight-year old. I would get extremely anxious at the thought of performing in a recital.

According to the Glossophobia website, public speaking is considered the greatest fear a person can have, for some even greater than the fear of death. A famous comedian once quipped at a funeral that "most people would rather be lying in the casket than delivering the eulogy." I wouldn't go that far, but I do understand the apprehension. Research shows that it is remarkably common, and that as many as 75% of us have some level of anxiety related to public speaking. In college, I would wait until the very last semester to take the required public speaking course. It was among the worst experiences of my life.

For the first ten or so years of teaching, my least favorite time of the year was the evening of Back-To-School Night, and the months long anticipation of it. I was somehow able to survive the evening by a combination of altering my state of consciousness and humor. Once I got my audience, the parents, laughing, I could begin to relax. I told them how fortunate I was to have great kids and great parents to work with (the truth), and when I perceived their inevitable prideful smiles, I knew that I was home free and was able to complete my presentation on automatic pilot. When I got to the question and answer portion, I would actually begin to enjoy myself. My biggest celebration of the year would commence after locking my classroom door that evening. I eventually began to almost look forward to this get-together as I derive pleasure from talking to parents about their kids.

Needless to say, THERE WAS ABSOLUTELY NO WAY IN THE WORLD THAT I WAS GOING TO ALLOW MY KIDS TO GO THROUGH WHAT I DID, the uneasiness, the anxiety because of an oral presentation. "You will not be disabled by this fear," I told them early in the year.

We started THE CURE gradually. Once a month (unless there was another oral project) we would memorize a poem, practicing in the classroom and hopefully at home in front of a family member or a mirror. About two weeks later, I would ask for volunteers to recite the poem to the class. Some kids enjoy performing, others just want to get it over with, and early in the year we might have five or six kids done the first day. Seeing their friends survive the ordeal, an equal number would volunteer the second day. Then came those who managed even though they were quite nervous, some needing an occasional prompt in sign language, a gesture, or verbal cue to get them back on track. Those who put off their task until the end are again reminded that NOBODY knows better than I how hard it is to get up there, how much courage it takes, but DON'T EVEN THINK OF GETTING OUT OF IT! Someone usually offered their parent's practical advice of picturing the audience naked or in their underwear, which would trigger a chorus of EWWWWWs and lighten up the group. I would suggest that one could focus on a spot just above the heads of the audience, that the speaker might be more comfortable, and those in the audience would not be aware of the lack of eye contact. We were now down to the most reluctant, anxious children, those who could be literally making themselves sick.

What worked best for the most reluctant kids, which may have worked for me, was the "teamwork" method. If a child wished, he/she could choose a friend, or two, half, or even the whole class to hold their hand or put arms around their shoulders for support. Some may even have been inspired by the tears they noticed forming in my eyes, happiness tears I would tell them, after a child broke out into the ubiquitous "smile of relief" upon completing their poem.

I received a signed note one day, just before our recitations were to begin:

"I JUST DON'T WANT TO   I AM AFRAID AND MY STOMACH TURNS UPSIDE DOWN
I REALLY WANT TO DO IT   BUT AM AFRAID"

P.S. She did it, WITH A LITTLE HELP FROM HER FRIENDS, and was able to do it again and again.

At the end of the year I would read out the names of the kids who had memorized and recited correctly all of the poems. Those that had an ALMOST perfect record often received the loudest and longest standing ovation, as their classmates understood that they had succeeded against what had first seemed like overwhelming odds. Of course, the largest smile was always mine.

In the decades that I required this, VERY few were not able to (eventually) recite all of the poems. I would add a line on their report card for POEMS (the only letter grade that they would receive). Almost every child could proudly say that they got an A on all of the poems, which translated to an A+ on their final grade. No administrator ever challenged this additional grade which was officially verboten.

I almost always started the year off with this slightly shortened version of a poem by Beatrice Schenk De Regniers:

KEEP A POEM IN YOUR POCKET
Keep a poem in your pocket
And a picture in your head
And you'll never feel lonely
At night when you're in bed.

The little poem will sing to you
The little picture bring to you
A dozen dreams to dance to you
At night when you're in bed.

One year, one of my multi-talented parents fashioned pockets for all of the students. This was a surprise as she had only volunteered to teach them how to sew on a button, a basic skill in my mind. A natural extension was to utilize these to temporarily house their monthly poem.

We would do other oral presentations, but the kids' (and my) favorite was the FAMOUS PEOPLE book report that we did in February. The kids chose a famous person, which could be (almost) anyone, as long as a book had been written about them. They would bring in the book for my approval, and I would write their name and famous person on the board along with their preferred presentation day, as motivation to find their book/person quickly so they could control the date (excited to perform, wanting to get it over with, somewhere in the middle, or put it off as long as possible).

After reading the book, the student would write or type an approximately two or three-page script, including the major benchmarks in the person's life, where and when they were born, their childhood, what they were known for, what they were doing now (or what they would be doing now if they were still alive). Many of the kids were interested in the cause of the person's death (Maybe they were CSI fans). They could read directly from the paper, a tablet, use 5 x 7 cards, or try to memorize sections, whatever they felt most comfortable with.

On the day of their presentation they would dress as this person and use appropriate props. Most kids enjoyed this assignment, both their own presentation and listening to the other celebrities. Very few had trouble performing including a few kids who were "selectively mute." They and other shy or glossophobic children seemed to be transformed that day, possibly because they were able to read their script, or maybe because as many shy/glossophobic actors admit, they are only able to perform when in character. Amazingly, this confidence seemed to stay with them for the rest of the day, or until they removed their "outfits."

After each guest spoke we would have a short period for compliments and questions. Parents were not allowed to attend these sessions as many of the children remarked that they got too nervous when others were in the audience. We did tape each performance and loaned out VHS tapes (in the early years), and later DVDs were provided for each participant.

It was a real honor meeting and questioning Charlie Chaplin, Queen Elizabeth, Amelia Earhart, the many sports figures and the others who visited our class, and fun getting to know them as real people. I would sometimes feel a tug at the heartstrings, or detect a moistening in the vicinity of my tear ducts when I saw Martin Luther King presented by a Caucasian girl, Abraham Lincoln by an African-American, or George Washington by an excited Muslim boy, but this doesn't seem to impact the kids. They understand innately that a hero doesn't come in sizes, colors, or genders.

We would "take the show on the road," reciting our poems, or whatever, for one of the kindergarten or first grade classes, maybe the principal (if he/she was accommodating), and almost always for the secretaries, who did more for my students' self-esteem than they can ever imagine.

The Famous People presentations became a tradition, and the kids were in such demand those days in February that the K, first and second-teachers would ask to be notified of the schedule. I would leave it up to the kids to get together with their former teacher or a sibling's teacher, and would help schedule only the new students.

As the year progressed, more and more children would volunteer to go first, and the sea of waving hands would make my day, my year! It would add to the feeling that perhaps I had found my life's calling.

Occasionally, I would summon the words of Professor Kingsfield (John Houseman) from the movie *The Paper Chase*, to encourage a shy child or the entire class:
"FILL THIS ROOM WITH YOUR INTELLIGENCE!"

16 READING

Some of my favorite times in elementary school were when it was pouring outside because then we would have to stay inside. After lunch, since the teachers didn't want to give up their break, a BIG KID (fifth or sixth-grader) would come to our classroom and read to us. I frequently hoped for Curious George.

Much of the day in early education is spent on reading, LEARNING TO READ, and then for the rest of our lives, READING TO LEARN. And yet, there are many, an estimated 10 to 20 percent, who never learn to read proficiently.

Many kids come to school reading. They have learned by one, or a combination of methods. Some pick it up effortlessly, almost by magic, and continue to add to their sight words and vocabulary daily. Some discover the code to reading words from having been read to, observing signs on their daily journeys, watching educational television or on their computer. Others credit the help of the alphabet, phonemic-awareness, and phonics.

One of my favorite approaches is through "experiential books" or stories. An adult, or older child, sits down with the young child and listens to their personal story. It could be the story of their short but interesting life, a pet, their family, what they like to do, fill in the blank. The person who is listening writes down what the child has dictated, in book form, which could be as simple as folding 8 ½ x 11 pieces of paper in half and stapling the spine. The child chooses a title, and might illustrate the book. It's great fun, exciting, and quite motivating, reading a story or book about your life, written by you!

Many across the country witnessed a major **"disruption"** in reading education back in the 80s. One day we were told to turn in all the books from our previous (phonics-based) reading series, and that henceforth we would be subscribing **ONLY** to the WHOLE LANGUAGE APPROACH. The majority of the teachers in **our** large urban school district, though mumbling, followed this edict.

The Whole Language Approach is a method of teaching reading "by recognizing words as whole pieces of language." Proponents opine that language "should not be broken down into letters and combinations of letters and decoded." In other words, they were opposed to the phonics approach. The new whole language readers were loaded with exciting, inspirational, beautiful literature, and I would utilize them as supplemental readers throughout my career. This method was not a problem for those children who already knew how to read, those who could learn by any method, or those who were in the Reading To Learn phase, but it was a tragedy for many children who required an alternative method to learn how to read. Decision makers in many districts across the nation somehow failed to understand that ONE SIZE DOES NOT FIT ALL. Teachers are intelligent enough and hopefully brave enough to disregard such ignorant mandates should the pendulum ever swing back that far again. They should be trusted to use all options until they find the one which works for each child.

Most children will learn to read without too much difficulty by second grade. Too often, the prescription for those who are having challenges with reading is to continue to give him or her more and more of the same technique which is not working. By third grade, the kids who are struggling become more obvious. Up until then, many get by with remarkable coping skills, memorizing long passages or using context clues such as observing illustrations to guess the words and their meanings. Many of these children would have been identified by kindergarten or first grade if teachers were taught what to observe.

During parent conferences for kids with learning "challenges," we often play the blame game, whose side of the family, which former teacher, school, was to blame. Often, I'd hear, "All of his/her teachers so far said that he/she was doing well." I would make the prediction that, eventually, we'll probably have brain scans to make a correct diagnosis/prognosis/ prescription. I frequently found myself saying, I WISH THAT I COULD CRAWL INTO THEIR BRAIN AND LOOK THROUGH THEIR EYES to know what they're seeing.

The year that approximately half of my 31 students had difficulties with reading, I knew that I would have to try something different. Sixteen of my students were having obvious challenges. There were 93 kids in the third grade, so that particular year almost 20% of those children were having problems.

Keep in mind that this was before computers were commonplace, before the sharing of knowledge on the internet was as popular as it is now. One morning while I was working with a small group of "challenged-readers," one of my students picked up a transparent, blue acetate sheet (which I was using as a cover for a report), and placed it over his open reader. I understand that these colored "overlays" are controversial, and many "experts" claim that they have no use in reading. Someone failed to tell this to my third grader, who jumped up and began dancing. "GEE, MR. A, READING'S A LOT MORE FUN WHEN YOU KNOW THE WORDS!" We experimented with other colors of the acetate sheets which I had available. I learned that a company was selling a set of (very expensive) sheets, in a variety of colors, and I purchased them. This company was also claiming that colored lens mounted in glasses would benefit some. I allowed the children to test all of the different colored overlays, and we determined that most of them made little difference, but occasionally one or two did.

Something came to me which seemed almost TOO SIMPLE. Many have certainly been doing this since the beginning of time, just no one that I knew. I began ASKING THE CHILDREN WHAT THEY SAW! Obvious, right? I thought so.

I would pull my students out individually and have them read a passage from our grade level reader. I'd then say something like, "Everyone sees things differently. For instance, when I look at that cloud out there, I see a fluffy rabbit." *"I see a dog,"* they might reply. I asked them if they ever got tired when they read (like I did when I was their age). We then looked at a different passage and I asked the child what they saw. I'm pretty sure, based on the looks that I got, that they had never been asked this question before. Here are some of the responses I got from my third graders, an age when most were able to articulate what they were seeing:

The (colored) marker helps me see better and read faster. It helps me concentrate. It makes the words "darker" so I can read better.

Sometimes I lose my place. My eyes get tired sometimes, and get blurry for a second, but then if I blink they get in focus.

Sometimes it kind of looks like I'm seeing double, when I'm reading or anytime. When I'm reading, the words kind of pop up, like 3-D. Sometimes the words "change backwards," and sometimes I skip words. With the (blue) marker, I don't skip words (sometimes) and I don't see 3-D. Sometimes my eyes go fuzzy and blurry.

The words split apart (vertically). When I look at them too long they get all white.

When I'm reading, my eyes go this way, "the opposite of cross-eyed," and it's hard for me to read. The letters get blurry. It doesn't make my eyes go blurry when I use the marker.

The marker helps because then my eyes don't fall down, and I don't lose my place.

Sometimes when I look at something, and I say it, the sentence comes out all messed-up.

The blue marker helps because it makes the words gentler, and without it the words are too bright.

The words look really small. When I am far away the words look all black.

The words are blurry. The word that's supposed to be AND looks like NAD. When I'm looking at a word the other words move up. The doctor said that I'm going to have an operation to fix my eyes.

The words look like in movies, how they go up and down. They're OK at first, but about here (pointing to the second paragraph) they start moving. My eyes get really tired.

The words are all moving in circles. Some are changing different colors. Some of the words move off the page. The (blue) marker stops them from moving.

I shared these with my vision therapist friend, and told her that these were some comments made by my students, describing what they saw when they attempted to read. *"How do you know this is what they saw?"* she inquired. "I ASKED THEM!" I responded. *"You **WHAT?**"* she questioned skeptically.

The "markers" that they were referring to were strips of colored overlays which I modified with two strips of fabric tape to form a horizontal window slightly larger than the print size. I, with the kids' direction, found that the colors which (sometimes) worked for them were the blue and the yellow. As I noted before, many experts say that these do not work, but if you ask my kids, and adults with whom I've shared, or me, who have benefitted from their use, we would disagree. From our experiences, the yellow often works for those who have trouble tracking (following with their eyes) or who are having trouble concentrating, those who continually lose their place, or find themselves re-reading the same passage over and over. The blue sometimes works (if only temporarily) for "other challenges." A colleague of mine (who wears prescription glasses) was able to read the phone book for the first time, once she was introduced to a blue marker.

If someone had asked me at age 8, 18, or even 28, I might have said, I can read anything pretty quickly for a while, then I kind of lose concentration (A.D.D.?) and might lose my place (even when I was reading music). I sometimes read the same line over and over, and eventually I'd get very tired. When I began working with the kids, I figured out that the solution for my problem was more practice, strengthening my "eye muscles." Now, I read about 200 or so books a year. If I find it difficult to focus because I have too much on my mind, or if I'm super tired, I occasionally use my (commercial) yellow highlighted marker until I can rid myself of some of the extraneous, tangential thoughts or get some rest.

I've supplied literally hundreds of these "markers" to my students, other children, and adults over the past few decades, and eventually purchased them in lots of three dozen. I once bought enough to share with all of the primary teachers at my school. I instructed them in their use, but did not repurchase them after I heard that they had been used as stocking-stuffers or handed out according to which color the child liked.

I am not claiming that these highlighted markers work for those with "dyslexia," or that they work for everyone with reading challenges. What I do say is that THEY HELP SOME PEOPLE, and that's good enough for me.

I recently offered my assistance in observing a younger child, a first grader, who was having problems reading. My approach was slightly different as she was younger than the kids that I had been working with, and we had never met. I introduced myself and told her that I was a teacher. I mentioned that my friend talks about her a lot (true), and often says how smart she is (true). I told her that I was interested in the way "smart" people see things (also true, I'm interested in how ALL people "see" things.). I was wondering if she would be able to help me with my project. She was very receptive, and cooperative, and I was able to determine some "obstacles" that might be impairing her ability to read. I also learned in the hour that I spent with her that she was very creative, a gifted artist, and an amazing dancer, and told her so.

I became aware that many of my students were having trouble when the surface of the reading material is high contrast (very black letters on a super-white paper). Possibly this is why the overlays, high-lighted windows, work for some. I noticed that the same was true when white boards became popular. The school district was not impressed with my recommendation (prior to renovation) of replacing the flickering fluorescent lights with full-spectrum lights (which imitated natural light) or uncovering the original skylights.

I tried to provide alternatives for those children who were disabled by what I (unscientifically) called glare. Other than the overlays/markers, we tried old-fashioned blackboards which are extremely hard to find. I realize that chalk is not the best idea for those with allergies, but many kids cheered and told me that it was so much easier to read. I also like using chalk for teaching cursive and calligraphy because the chalk against the board has a certain feel, more forgiving, and almost soulful.

Some of the children prefer lower contrast papers for duplicated materials, turning on/off certain banks of lights, closing/adjusting the curtains during different times of the day, and were thankful that I allowed them to choose their seating according to the lighting conditions which worked best for them.

My father helped me construct some desk easels which held a book, and allowed the child to adjust the reading angle to their comfort/glare level. There were enough for everyone, and whether or not they used one was totally up to them.

For those who continued to have challenges, I would suggest a trip to the optometrist/ophthalmologist to eliminate the possibility of acuity or other visual problems.

Let me pause for a second to say that I'm not claiming any credit for any of these ideas or devices, I'm simply sharing some of the things which worked for some of my kids over the years. Others will be able to tell you (scientifically) why they work, don't work, or why I am wrong and foolish.

With the kids who appeared "overwhelmed" by the amount of words on the page, I would cut a piece of black tag board to a size which covered the particular page. I would then cut out a window, one third of the way down the page, the width slightly more than the print size, and slightly longer than the sentence. This would isolate one sentence at a time, which made it more manageable for some. For others I would tape a colored overlay strip to the back of the window, occasionally using a double layer for those who felt that a darker color worked for them.

A small number of my kids tried vision therapy for visual tracking and vision perception skills. One therapist trained me over a full-weekend, and I would utilize this training when I had the time or help, limiting my scope to tracking and saccadic eye movement (rapid eye movements with constantly changing foci) exercises. An example of a tracking exercise would be, given a line of different shapes (or letters), the child would follow the line from left to right in a continuous motion with their eyes and a pencil, searching for and looping (in a counter-clockwise direction), the designated shape or letter.

Until the fire marshal forbid me, I would hang, 10 to 15, (different color) copies of the same 2-D object from the ceiling, at different heights and depths. Several times each day, I would halt what we were doing to instruct the children to find (focus on) a green ___, a blue___, a... Hopefully, some of these exercises benefitted some, and didn't hurt any.

At the first parent conference, I would ask the parents of a reading-challenged child if there had been any history of ear infections, to determine if an auditory discrimination weakness could be a culprit. The years that I was fortunate enough to have help in the afternoon from an enthusiastic morning kindergarten teacher, we would experiment (with varying levels of success) with miscellaneous programs, including an Orton-Gillingham based program intended for those with dyslexia.

At the time I entered teaching, dyslexia was used as a generic term for those who had trouble reading. A popular theory was that dyslexics saw things differently, often in reverse. This made sense when one noticed the number of dyslexics who are architects, designers, and artists, and that many of them reverse letters and numbers, that some (Leonardo da Vinci) write in what we might call mirror-writing. One of my students, in class, made an amazingly accurate rendering of his backyard (His parents later shared photos with me) from an aerial view. Other dyslexics among my young students were incredibly creative musicians, artists, dancers, and actors. One, with a bit of guidance, could have interned as a house framer, had she felt the desire.

Today, with the use of brain imaging, many researchers are looking at the language processing area for answers. There are plenty of books on dyslexia, with many different viewpoints, so I will not spend too much time on this subject except to express a few opinions, suggestions:

While they are learning to read, make sure that the "reading challenged" are not missing out on **any** of the lessons, not only in reading but the other subjects as well… math, science, social science… They should be listening to CDs or to others who are reading the lesson to them. I've found that most of these children don't have problems with their comprehension, only their reading.

I'm not a techie, but I'm sure that someone by now has created a device which will scan a page and read the text back to the user. When I first saw, heard my cousin talking to SIRI, I asked if one could take a picture and ask her to read it back. Not only did this appear to be possible, but the rate of speed at which SIRI read the words evidently could be adjusted. Let's utilize and share any available apps and devices which might be beneficial to our kids (and adults).

No child should be losing out, falling behind in any academic area because they can't read (with their eyes). Until they can read with adequate fluency, allow them to read "with their ears," including on their tests.

Let's not cheat a child, or the world, of their brilliant ideas because we (educators and society) are uninformed, misinformed, lazy, or stuck in the past.

Likewise, if a child is having difficulties getting their phenomenal ideas down on paper, consider allowing them to use a word recognition software program, or at least let them dictate their thoughts to an adult or classmate. You're already aware of their weakness, are working towards a solution, but in the interim, aren't you interested in hearing what they have to say?

THE BEST EVER READING PROGRAM
(And How to Improve On It)

One might reason that reading programs should continue to get better and better over the ages, as we collaborate with others, note what works, heed the research. This has not been the case in my experience. The best reading program which I have ever seen was the one at my first school, approximately four decades ago.

There was a reading teacher at my school who may not have had the best "bedside manner," but I'm pretty sure she could have taught my dog how to read. Early in the school year, all of the first through third grade teachers got together (volunteered is too strong a word) for a full weekend to create teacher-made reading games and other materials. During that weekend, and in the weeks to come, I learned along with the kids, about phonemes, phonemic awareness, word families… the basics of reading.

We were fortunate to have the funds to hire a few amazing aides who would "drill" the kids, and take them through a sequence of our teacher-created lessons which complemented the reading series. They often reminded the children how lucky they were, how thankful they should be that they had a teacher who cared about them, and that they were able to attend school. People around the world aren't all so fortunate. All first and second-grade students were pulled out individually to an adjacent room where they would play reading games and read related practice sentences which took them from the short through the long vowels, blends through the schwa — Those who got it quickly were out for only a few minutes, those who had difficulties were pulled out more often UNTIL THEY GOT IT. We worked together as a team, and DID NOT ALLOW ANYONE TO FALL BETWEEN THE CRACKS!

Since our school had top priority in transportation (bussing), we were able to benefit from early/late classes. Half of the children would come at 8:00 and leave at 2:30, the other kids would begin school at 9:00 and stay until 3:30. This allowed us to work with "only" 15 or 16 students during reading instruction, the first and last hours of the day.

The children were assigned to a group depending on their reading ability. They were **not** labeled the "bluebirds" or the "redbirds," and they were happy because they were reading at their level, challenged, and not struggling. They were aware that they could move between groups should their skills improve.

We were blessed to have a "resource specialist" who trusted our judgment. If we had a child we thought might have a learning challenge, we didn't wait until they were far behind to have them assessed. She would screen them and if they needed additional help she would provide it.

If I were in charge, I would build on one similar to this very successful program. I would create district TEAMS OF SPECIALISTS in Reading and Math, with possibly an OCCUPATIONAL THERAPIST, who would SCREEN ALL OF THE CHILDREN IN THE DISTRICT who were having difficulties at the first, second, and third-grade levels. This team would ASSESS, DIAGNOSE, AND MAKE SUGGESTIONS as to what would benefit these kids, and we would follow through with their recommendations.

We would create programs to meet their needs. If we are not willing (or able) to fund these necessary programs as a district, a state, or a nation, we should approach corporations, write grants, or open a "fund me" account online. If the community knew what we were doing, they would, I am sure, be willing to help.

17 MATH

"Don't play what's there, play what's not there."
— Miles Davis

Playing what's there maintains the status quo—MEDIOCRITY. Play (teach) from your heart, your **SOUL**, not from some bland, safe, boring script intended for the masses! Play (teach) what's possible for each child!

Recent studies are telling us that a large percentage of lower elementary (primary) teachers are afraid of teaching Math, and therefore rely solely on the district-adopted textbook to address the needs of the students. Let's hope that this isn't the case. Tons of ideas and resources for teaching math exist online so I'll just offer a few observations.

Children should be introduced at a young age to manipulatives (the concrete) before we can expect them to transition to the abstract world of numbers. Before using them in the lesson, allow the kids time to play with them, get their "ya-ya's out," before they get down to serious work.

The Japanese, who have very successful math programs, readily admit that they "borrowed" many of the ideas from us. They are utilizing some of the methods we once used before they were seemingly discarded, perhaps because they required some thought, and a bit of extra effort. Instead of reading along with the scripted math book, and providing the student with ONE CORRECT WAY of doing a problem, consider presenting the problem and then challenging the kids to come up with the solution using any method they choose. Have volunteers explain how they came up with their answer, and discuss each approach. How many did it this way? Who did it another way? Which method do you think you might use if you had a similar problem in the future? Don't *assume* that kids understand, and don't tell them what YOU think they're thinking, ASK THEM WHAT THEY'RE THINKING (check for understanding). You may want to have them explain their thoughts in writing. Be gentle if you must correct their ideas so they feel good about speaking up down the road.

Provide your students with practical, real world challenges which they can relate to so that they understand why learning Math is so important, and that IT CAN BE FUN. At the end of each chapter or section, consider doing a related project, especially if the children seem unsure of a concept, are weak in a particular area. If they continue to have trouble with measurement after you've measured a number of lines, objects, distances indoors and outside, you might build a small stool or toolbox for use in the classroom, or a doghouse to auction off as a fundraiser. If you're not comfortable with the tools, the process, enlist the services of a parent or other volunteer. Hands-on, practical work reinforces the concept which was previously only words and theory.

My kids enjoyed the "egg carton challenge," which I borrowed from a presenter/author at a math workshop. "My friend, a farmer, is looking for some novel designs for the cartons she will use for her chicken eggs. She would like you to design some which will house six (a half-dozen), twelve (a dozen), and twenty-four (2 dozen). The rules are that the cartons must be one layer and rectangular."

"Using our multi-link cubes (manipulatives), come up with all the possibilities for 6, 12, and 24 eggs, draw them on the graph paper and label them. Cut out all the options for each amount and paste them on a separate piece of paper." They are learning the basics of multiplication (arrays) in a practical way. Explain to them that, for instance, for the two by three solution we write 2 x 3, and say two times three equals six (2 x 3 =6).

"Circle the ones that you think that Farmer Jones should consider, and explain the reasons for your choice." After a week or so, I reward them with marshmallow eggs for their efforts.

Utilize MNEMONICS to help remember procedures or sequences. For long division, try **d**ad, **m**om, **s**ister, **b**rother (or **d**irty **m**arsupials **s**mell **b**ad) for divide, multiply, subtract, bring down. Kids love to make these up, and will have better recall if they own the prompt.

Teach them the little tricks, such as multiplying "the nines" using one's fingers. Put both hands in front of you (palms down), numbering the fingers (from the left) 1 through 10. Bend whatever number (finger) you are multiplying by 9. If I were multiplying 9 times 8, I would bend over my right middle finger. Everything to the left of the bent finger is multiplied by ten (the number in the tens' column), and everything to the right is in the ones' column. Thus, 7 tens and two ones equal 72. (9 x 8=72)

You may want to look into integrating movement and math as done in the Waldorf schools.

Teach the kids HOW TO THINK with a sequential unit on LOGIC.

Take advantage of current technology to utilize interactive math lessons, activities, and tutorials.

Provide a comfortable, functional environment which allows the children flexibility of movement to collaborate on solutions.

18 WRITING

I trust that the school/district where you are employed has discovered and is utilizing an excellent writing program which has been proven to work with kids. Most children (people) are not "naturals" and must be taught how to write. Giving a writing assignment without instruction is asking for failure and frustration.

Encourage the students to come up with their own ideas of what they'd like to write about and keep track of these in a notebook or a page in their journal. These might feature their interests, personal experiences, what's going on in their world. Brainstorm as a group to generate other interesting topics. Add these and others as they are spawned to a visible class list.

BIG FAT JUICY SENTENCES

An idea which worked well for teaching my students to write more interesting sentences was called Expanding Sentences (which I would change to BIG, FAT, JUICY SENTENCES). Starting with a basic sentence containing a noun, verb, and an article, we would make the sentence more exciting by incrementally adding adjectives, adverbs, prepositional phrases, and adverbial phrases and clauses. Visualize the cues inked on the digits of a hand, WHO, WHAT, WHERE, WHEN, WHY.

The dog dug would become The young dog dug, The lonely, young dog dug, The lonely, young dog dug indiscriminately... eventually expanding to something like Whenever its master left, the lonely, young dog dug indiscriminately in the backyard because she was bored and had nothing else to do.

We would revisit the lesson periodically, pinning our BIG, FAT, JUICY SENTENCES on a bulletin board for all to enjoy.

SOME WRITING BASICS

Here are a few standards, known to most but often neglected because of a perceived lack of time:

Journaling

Take five or ten minutes a day, perhaps the first thing in the morning, to jot down in a designated notebook your current feelings, something that happened yesterday or that you plan to do today, what you're looking forward to in the future, a new idea that you can't wait to write about, something which has been bothering you, a dream you had, a dream you have for the world, or a prompt your teacher has asked you to consider. The contents of these journals should be semi-confidential, and the private information shared only if deemed necessary.

I Am Grateful

Another daily (or weekly) journal in which one chronicles one thing (or person) for which (whom) they are thankful, that they appreciate. This is sometimes difficult for a young child because, like the rest of us, they often take things, people, for granted. If they are unable to provide an entry on a particular day (they may feel pressured, have brain freeze, or have simply run out of ideas), allow them to repeat something (someone) they've mentioned previously or to acknowledge the fundamental life forces of breathing, a beating heart, or... their hands. Be careful, they can easily get carried away with various body parts.

On the occasional "down" day, a child may want to revisit these many "up" times which have been affirmed in their "Grateful Journal."

POETRY

Here are some common forms of poetry which might help a child's self-image:

Acrostic

The acrostic poem spotlights the child's name which is spelled out vertically. In the simplest version, each letter of the name becomes the first letter for a line of the poem.

Memories of friends and family are most important
Always doing for, or thinking about others
Ready, at the drop of a hat, to help
Years of pleasant experiences knitting with kids

Me, From A to Z

Using the alphabet poem format (hopefully all 26 letters), the students are encouraged to share themselves with others, exploring their strengths, weaknesses, likes, dislikes…

Always trying to just be myself
Zoos are where I like to spend as much time as possible

Self-Cinquain

As the name implies, this is a five-line poem with the following formula:

Line 1   one word, usually a noun, that names the subject (in this case the child)
Line 2   two adjectives which describe the subject in line 1
Line 3   three "ing" words which also describe the subject
Line 4   a phrase or sentence about the noun in line 1
Line 5   a word or two (or so) that rename the noun in line 1

> Portia
> Shy, friendly
> Listening, helping, laughing
> Eager to learn French
> Named after a car!

Self-Simile

Discuss the definition of "simile". A simile uses figurative language to compare two different things using the words LIKE or AS. Brainstorm a list of character, personality, and physical traits (caring, thoughtful, stubborn, nervous…). Ask the student to choose 6-10 (or so) of these qualities, and construct similes which describe themselves.

Patient as a kindergarten teacher
Talkative like a teenager on social media
Curious as a cat
Generous like a fruit tree

Alliteration

In the vein of the book *Animalia*, write an ABC or free-form alliteration book where each letter in the sentence (if possible) begins with the same sound. With a partner, or in a small group, the children may choose their own theme. Allow them to use "dictionaries."

All armadillos abhor artichokes.
Princely peacocks prance presumptuously.

Thank-you Notes

PLEASE teach your students how to write thank-you notes and educate them that the recipients, those who have done something *for them*, will greatly appreciate this thoughtful, courteous, considerate, well-mannered effort. Convince them that it is the right thing to do.

A Wish List

For a writing assignment, I often have kids tell me what they would do if they were the president, the king, queen, the principal, what they would change, get rid of, make happen, even if it took a magic wand. Included near the top of *my* list would be an INTERNATIONAL SIGN LANGUAGE, taught in all schools, which consisted of gestures to include basic greetings, common phrases, and survival, emergency vocabulary which people of all nations would recognize. YES, I AM A DREAMER.

"I'll let you be in my dreams if I can be in yours."
— Dylan

I tell my reluctant writers to pretend that they are talking to their most-trusted best friend. Just think what you want to tell them, and now, write that down!

VOCABULARY

Expose your kids to more challenging, interesting vocabulary. Introduce a "word of the day" which is, along with its definition, written on the board, "framed," or written out and kept in their pocket to be visited during the day.

As a group, make up a short story which includes the new word and also explains and reinforces its definition.

A game most of my students enjoyed which seemed to bolster their memories was, using an old-fashion dictionary or electronic device, answer the following, supporting your answer:

Can a gargoyle gargle? Does a waffle have a wattle? Which is more sanguinary, a vampire or a verandah? Would you take a dare and climb into a maw? (I borrowed these from an unknown source, but also enjoyed making up my own so I could control the vocabulary).

Encourage the children to share the new vocabulary, stories, and challenges with their families the same evening. Besides enriching the entire family's vocabulary, as with all new knowledge or skills, the more one is exposed, practices in the initial twenty-four period, the greater chance that they will retain it.

KITES

One of the most popular, fun, and successful projects we ever did was the KITES. We adults must do much of the preparation work, and the students have most of the fun, but it is "off the charts" rewarding to witness their creativity, excitement, and satisfaction. Everyone needs a break occasionally from academics, and I don't know of a better way than getting out in the fresh air and watching something that you produced soar 400 feet into the heavens.

Kites were the finale to our poetry unit. On a day in early March, I would announce that we would be writing a poem the following day, that they might want to think between now and then about the following subject. There would be the inevitable moans and groans, and I would console them. "Oh, you don't have to write this poem if you don't want to!" A few muffled cheers would be heard.

"If you choose not to do this, I will give you an alternate project. Those who write the poem will copy it onto the kites that we will soon fly." Most would be convinced to give it a try, and when they heard what we would be writing about, the rest were converted. We would often write a scaffolded poem about what their future life would be like. The children enjoyed writing these and their parents enjoyed reading them. They make predictions about college, married life, kids, where they would live, their profession, future vehicles, etc. The form of the poem is simple couplets, the first line being WHEN I GROW UP, and the second I WILL.

> When I grow up I will live in Seattle.
> I will live in a houseboat on the water.

> When I grow up I will go to Harvard.
> I will major in art.

I would have the kite (made from a white garbage bag) cut out, with the dowels taped on (the margins of our writing). They would copy their completed poem with a sharpie-type marker, using a ruler as a guide for the baseline. When they completed the poem, and had passed my editing, they could illustrate and decorate the kite with colored markers. I would then complete the kite, taping on the leader, providing them with a ball of string and tails (crepe paper streamers in a variety of colors).

We would then watch the weather and the flag for the perfect breeze, and if it was not during a "sacred" time, I would pass out the folded, already prepared kites, and we would quickly evacuate the room. For many, this was their first experience with kites so I would give a quick demo on flying, warn them not to let the kite go, and to stay away from the trees and wires. We would, for a half hour or so, forget about school, and with very few exceptions, all would be successful.

A BASIC KITE REPAIR KIT is a necessity: scissors, (strapping) tape, tissues for the occasional tears of the impatient and those awaiting kite repair.

My students were always good about sharing their kites with our kindergarten friends and others whom we would invite to join us.

I sometimes hung the kites on our clotheslines for Open House before we took them home. One year, one of my students entered her unmodified kite in a city contest and won first place for highest flying kite.

Kite Instructions

On a white heavy-duty garbage bag, trace around a full-size tagboard pattern, or fold the bag over and use the half-size pattern. Cut out the kite with sharp scissors, an x-acto knife, or a rotary cutter. Saw a 36-inch long, 1/8-inch dowel in half and attach both resultant pieces with strapping tape (fold over the tape and secure it on both sides) as shown (A).

Tape the two ends of a 4-foot sturdy, medium-weight string leader at point B on the side opposite the dowels. With the leader on the dowel side, tie a small loop at the mid-point, and attach the kite string with several secure knots. If you wish, you may add colorful crepe paper streamers for tails. This will not positively or negatively affect the flight of the kite, but will add to the oohs and the aahs.

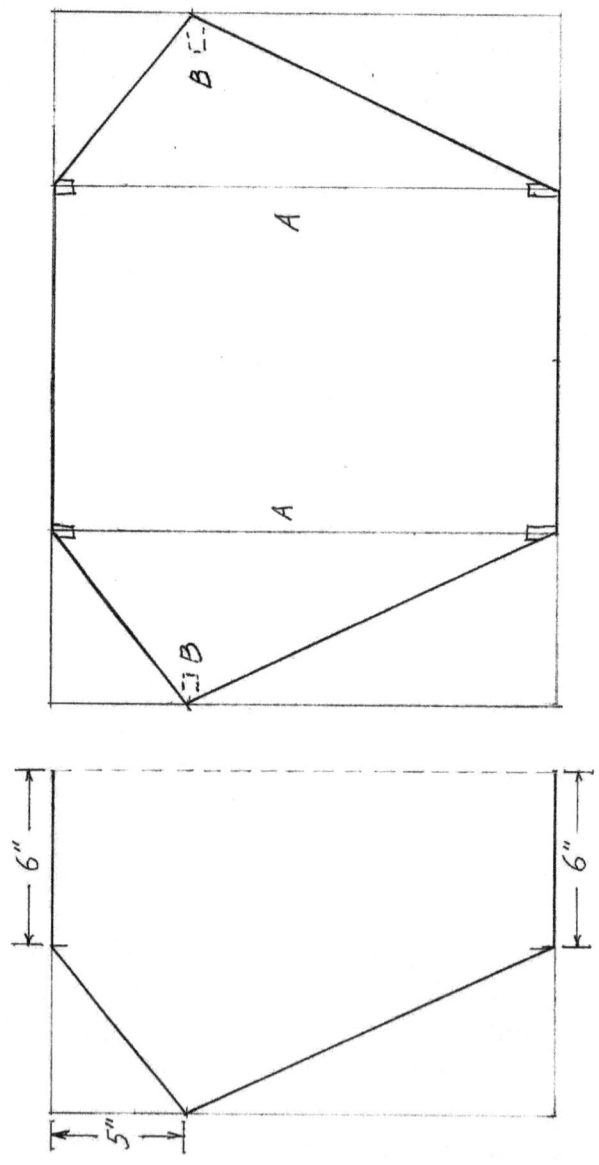

If you don't feel you have the time or energy for kites, consider instead writing the poem on a piece of standard-size paper, and using online instructions (or letting the kids design their own), turn it into the perfect paper airplane. Spend some time (indoors or out) flying the planes, before sharing the poems with the group.

PEN PALS

Consider having pen pals, writing buddies, from another school in the area, one with which you might be able to rendezvous on a field trip, maybe one from another part of the country, or from a foreign country, possibly one which you've been studying in class. This is quite practical and easy via e-mail, but can be even more exciting when using snail mail. Imagine receiving a decorated envelope with a colorful stamp from a far-off country, a chance to view your pal's handwriting, a bit of their personality, perhaps written in a different language, along with its translation into English. You may gain a friend for life, one whom you could someday visit or invite to visit you. You might even be motivated to learn a new foreign language. Kids are often the best ambassadors, representatives for their countries.

BOOK REPORTS

My students were assigned monthly (hopefully fun) book reports. The first one of the year could be as simple as creating a book jacket along with three paragraphs summarizing the book, what happened at the beginning, middle, and end of the story. Another might be a blog article discussing the book with one's friends.

One of our favorites was the "animal book report." The children were asked to discover as much information as possible, reading books, articles, whatever, about an animal of their choice. Their challenge was to create a RESTAURANT MENU where the animal might be excited to eat breakfast, lunch, or dinner. The child was required to name the restaurant, determine the location, food (appetizers, entrees, desserts, beverages), and monetary unit (sand dollars?), based on the animal's habitat, diet, and routines. We all enjoyed reading these so much that many were visibly upset when I removed them from the board to send home.

19 ARTS & MUSIC

Standing in line at a grocery store, I heard this familiar admission: *"If it wasn't for art and music, my years in school would have been a catastrophe."*

Besides the lifelong pleasure one receives from creating, performing, listening to, or viewing art, music, or dance, the arts do so much more. An arts program in school has been shown to not only increase achievement in the basics of reading and math, but also to enhance one's verbal, cognitive, and critical thinking skills.

The thrill, the sense of accomplishment one receives from building a pinch pot, drawing a self-portrait, painting a watercolor landscape, accompanying a recording with rhythm instruments, conceiving a new composition on a xylophone (using a pentatonic scale where everyone is successful), playing a recorder or ukulele, or executing a free form dance, has incalculable benefits. It gives one motivation to work harder on academics, increases focus (concentration), as it boosts confidence and self-esteem. It stimulates creativity, and gives the child a reason to work, collaborate, to connect with others.

The arts engage, involve, some who might be having difficulties surviving in a traditional education system. It gives many who may not otherwise have a channel to express themselves, a way to communicate their feelings, their emotions in an appropriate, acceptable way.

I don't remember when I ceased being surprised that it was so often those children who had academic challenges who were among the most capable in creating an incredible work of art, playing an instrument remarkably well, performing an exceptionally graceful dance, or bringing a character alive in a class play.

I believe that maintaining an arts curriculum in the schools is not only wise, but should be mandatory.

ARTIST OF THE MONTH

The ARTIST OF THE MONTH was one of the methods I utilized for introducing my students to art and artists. Many hours were spent accumulating art books, detaching the spine, trimming and laminating the photos of the artist's work. This is a large investment in both time and money, so I would suggest that you peruse used book stores, seek out donations of art books which may be sitting around the house, and recruit volunteers to help with the labor.

I create an aesthetically-pleasing arrangement of the artist's representative work, provide the students with a basic biography of their life, a geography lesson, where they were born, where they created their work, and interesting facts about them. I encourage the kids to visit this "gallery" when they are finished with their work, at lunch recess, or whenever they have the opportunity.

We often begin with Van Gogh. He is very popular with the kids, perhaps because many of them believe that they can do as well or better than he. Many are familiar, intrigued, grossed-out with a story of his missing ear. Near the end of the month, we do an art project related to the artist's style, subject, or medium. In the case of Van Gogh, we might draw our dream bedroom, do a (directed lesson) self-portrait, or design a chair. The original art work created by the students, I thought, was often as interesting as that of the artist's.

Other artists and projects enjoyed by my kids were: Leonardo da Vinci (children as inventors), Monet, Mary Cassatt (women and children), Escher (kid-created tessellations t-shirts), Jean-Michel Basquiat ("kid-like" sketches), Georgia O'Keefe (large pastel flowers), Hiroshige (the great wave, printmaking), Warhol or Oldenburg (common objects), Frida Kahlo (fun self-portraits), Romare Bearden (collage), Picasso…

Local artists can be interesting and exciting because the children can relate to them as real (living) people, may choose to write to them, visit them in their studio, or possibly persuade them to visit your classroom.

I choose a variety of artists, making sure that women are represented as well as the ethnic backgrounds of my children. If this is a school/district-wide program, you would want to plan so the children are exposed to different artists each year.

A school-wide (actually K-3) project I will "never forget," are the murals that all of the children took part in. Each time they viewed these they would smile, feel a great deal of pride, and were able to say, "*I helped make that!*" Your choices of medium could include paint, hand-made ceramic tiles, or baker's dough.

MUSIC

No teacher has an excuse for not including *some* music in the day, even if it is simply listening to a survey of different types of music played on an electronic device. I played everything from ABBA to ZAP MAMA (not Zappa), choosing genres which I thought the children would not ordinarily listen to, when they were entering, exiting the room, and sometimes during art period or knitting.

At the very least we can use the (original) instrument which almost all of us inherited as standard equipment, our voice.

Jessye Norman, gospel and opera singer, offers:

> *"Singing for me is actually life itself. It's communication person to person, and soul to soul…*
>
> *It makes you feel good and it makes the person listening to you feel good as well."*

20 YOU MIGHT CONSIDER

You might consider some of the following for the fitness of your students' bodies and minds:

Waterfall/Fountain

For a peaceful, calming background noise, a waterfall or fountain (with recirculating water) may be just what the doctor (or therapist) ordered.

Zen Garden

A portable zen garden with sand, some well-placed rocks (stones), or other aesthetically pleasing objects, is a nice place to chill after a stressful or emotional lesson, task or testing period.

Juggling

Juggling is great for brain and body fitness, stress-relief, improving coordination, developing focus (concentration), confidence, and it's so fun that one doesn't even realize they are exercising. A suggestion… plan your scarf juggling on a mild day when the fan for the heater or air-conditioner is not running. The air movement makes it much more difficult to catch, throw, or control a meandering bandanna.

Speed Stacks

One of the most motivational and popular activities in my class was Speed Stacks. Great examples can be found on YouTube. My kids knew that if everyone finished all of their work early, we might spend the last 10 or 15 minutes on Speed Stack competitions. A student could challenge another willing student to a race, or they could choose to be involved in an elimination tournament, which took very little time because each match lasted only a few seconds! Besides being a physical and mental workout, it is great for crossing the mid-line of their body, and forming new connections in both hemispheres. It is also a good activity for increasing one's focus/concentration as well as their ambidexterity. Most kids achieve a boost in their confidence, their self-esteem, and we are often surprised when a seemingly "less athletic" child beats an "athlete."

Then there is   DANCE   TAI CHI   YOGA   BRAIN GYM   MEDITATION   ANY MOVEMENT ACTIVITIES.

FREE TIME

Some suggestions for "free time" activities, rainy days, so no child can ever say that there is nothing to do:

Commercial games (educational), for instance, Connect Four, Guess Who, checkers, chess

Hand Clap (a book of hand-clapping games)

Cat's Cradle (Klutz)… Each of the kids has a loop of string (satin cord) about 5 feet long, tied at the ends, and can learn to make constructions such as Witch's Broom, Jacob's Ladder, Eiffel Tower, Cup and Saucer.

Klutz Book of Knots… With 18-inch nylon cords (ends melted), the kids learn useful hitches, ties, wraps, and knots.

The rule for these activities is, after you've learned a new clap, string configuration, or knot, you are required to teach it to at least one other child (and they do likewise).

Puzzles, including maps of the United States, The World, etc.

Soma cube puzzles… I made enough, using recycled ½ inch wooden "unit" cubes from math manipulatives and Elmer's glue, so that each child could keep one at their desk.

Knitting was always encouraged, weaving only when we were working on a project.

A diagram of the 206 bones in our body was available for those so inclined. We had a skeleton and each child was required to learn at least 20 bones, from the cranium down to the phalanges.

For those who enjoyed doing research on the computer (or the old-school encyclopedia), I provided a list of 20 questions, the themes of which were determined by the particular month.

Hundreds of books on diverse topics, and in a variety of genres.

BUDDIES

Children often make the best teachers. Whether it is that they have a better rapport with other kids, they "speak the same language," or because of their more limited vocabulary they are able to speak at a kid's level, children are able to talk to their younger peers so they get it.

Why not take advantage of this resource and create a buddy system for tutoring, helping younger children to understand a new concept, being a big brother or sister, a "big friend," or just someone to talk to on occasion. This symbiotic relationship, a hero and someone receiving help, is a no-brainer.

For a school-wide program, teams of first-fourth, second-fifth, third-sixth, and any level and kindergarten work well. The obvious subjects which are conducive to teaming are Reading and Math (including drilling on facts), but any subject is possible. Our third-grade class once learned the fundamentals of the Constitution from a seventh-grade government class. Another time I loaned my solar kits to an eighth-grade science class and my students were rewarded with lessons on solar vehicles. A solar cookout with all the buddies in the school was fun. We sometimes took our "special needs" buddies on our full-day outdoor education field trip.

The obvious benefactor of the buddy system is the younger child, and of course that child's teacher. Never minimize the pride, self-worth and confidence gained by the older child when they help another.

CUSHIONS

Logan was a child who had difficulties getting started each morning. One day, I began moving my fist in a clock-wise circular motion on his back, telling him that I was going to "wind him up" every day. He laughed, seemed to enjoy the touch, and (for whatever reason) this appeared to work for a while. Another thing that worked for him (and others) was THE CUSHION, which I had read benefits some kids, especially those with "sensory integration dysfunction."

A parent, who enjoyed sewing, wanted to help the class in whatever way she could. I took her up on the offer, and asked if she could make a half-dozen, one inch thick, 12" x 12" foam cushions with corduroy covers. Several days later they arrived, even nicer than I had imagined as she constructed them with a kind of pocket (there's probably a name for this) which allowed the foam to be removed so the cover could be washed.

These worked well for several kids, especially Logan, but he soon stopped using it. I eventually figured out that he felt "singled-out." To avoid this "stigma" in the future, I teamed with my friend, colleague, and special education teacher extraordinaire, to make enough cushions for her students and mine. I purchased the materials (heavier corduroy this time, and denser foam), and cut out the foam, using an electric knife I found at a garage sale. She cut the corduroy and sewed the "pocketed" cushions.

Beginning the next year, all of our students would have the choice to use the cushions or not. If they weren't interested, or if they tried them and decided they didn't work for them, nothing was said. They were stored on a shelf in the back of the room, should anyone change their mind. They were quite popular with adults at Back-To-School Night, even before I asked them,

"How did *you* enjoy sitting on a hard chair for six hours a day when you were their age?"

One of my all-time favorite kids (tied for first with the rest of the children), a very bright, creative, clever, funny (in a good way) child came to our class with a bad reputation. Her former teachers claimed that she was often silly, and would fall off her chair. I witnessed this, and also noticed that this made her uncomfortable. She would pretend to be silly rather than having people think that she had trouble sitting in her chair. She chose to use a cushion, stopped falling off her chair and being silly, but she retained all of the other traits which made her the interesting, fun person that she will always be.

Some children nowadays might prefer the (much more expensive) commercial "tactile" cushions.

A CLASS GARDEN
IN A GARDEN DE VIDA (INNA GADDA DA VIDA),
a shout-out to IRON BUTTERFLY fans

You might be surprised how many children aren't knowledgeable about where their food comes from! Consider starting a garden. I was fortunate, for several years, to have the school garden right outside our classroom door. Besides the obvious, vegetables to eat, the beauty of the flowers, the intangible bounties are countless. There's something therapeutic about watching things grow which always seems to raise your spirits, make everything better.

When someone is having a rough day (or a great day), the chance to go into the garden and think, work off your angst, or just to meditate, is rejuvenating. Working outside in nature, getting away from the stresses of life, digging in the forgiving soil, planting seeds which will one day become a snack or part of a meal—all is good.

A project which I (and my kids) enjoyed was to scatter "garden quotes" among the vegetables in our plot. We would tear paper grocery bags into maybe 4 x 12 inch rectangles, on which we would write a quote, possibly decorate it, and then staple it onto a wooden stake to be buried in the dirt. The children could choose from a list of quotes I had collected from people much more expressive than I, use another favorite, or make up one of their own.

> *I perhaps owe having become a painter to flowers.*
> —Claude Monet
>
> *If you have a garden and a library, you have everything you need.*
> —Cicero
>
> *A book is a garden carried in the pocket.*
> —Chinese Proverb
>
> *Where flowers bloom, so does hope.*
> —former first lady, Lady Bird Johnson
>
> *All the flowers of all the tomorrows are in the seeds of today.*
> —Indian Proverb
>
> *Flowers always make people better, happier, and more helpful; They are sunshine, food, and medicine for the soul.*
> —Luther Burbank
>
> *A garden is a friend you can visit anytime.*
> —Unknown
>
> *The earth laughs in flowers.*
> —Ralph Waldo Emerson

One year we successfully grew marankas, interesting, gnarly, aesthetically-pleasing gourds, with nature-provided handles, and made them into shakers to play with our "marimbas." Another year we grew bird-house gourds and turned them into their namesake.

Consider building a frame loom for the entry to the garden... a rectangle, maybe 3 x 5 feet, constructed with 2 x 4s, supported by two 4 x 4s sunk in the ground with decorative copper caps. Ours swiveled, and was movable up and down (three different holes). Hammer nails or make notches, approximately one inch apart, across top and bottom of the frame. Wrap cotton string around the frame (the warp), and allow the children, parents, the community to weave in the weft (fill) composed of found twigs, driftwood, fabric scraps, their favorite novelty yarns, whatever, to create a unique, one-of-a-kind outdoor tapestry for all to share and enjoy.

How about having the children take photographs of the "bounties of the garden," and make them into greeting cards for a fundraiser?

Every garden needs a bench, a place to pause and rest, have a bite to eat, a conversation with a friend, work on an assignment, or simply to take in the beauty of nature.

Make sure that you involve the parents and the rest of the community. At some point, you might need help with the weeding, watering, and neighborhood watch.

21 HAND WORK

Former students who came back to visit, reminisce, occasionally thanked me for helping them learn to read, do math, or write stories. What I heard from them more often was how—building that stool introduced me to my love of wood, and helped inspire me to become a finish carpenter—they still had the jump rope that they braided (the one that I had mentioned they might want to pass on to their kids and grand-kids)—doing art made the rest of the school subjects bearable—they built on those skills and were using them in their profession—ceramics is now the hobby which keeps them centered, and fills all of their "leisure time"—not only did they maintain their love of weaving, but they were now spinning their own wool—they were "pretty sure" that they'd be knitting for the rest of their life, and that they had never had a boring day since learning this skill (I heard the word "tactile" a lot.)—their art had made them "feel good inside" back then, and that that good feeling and the love of art have never gone away.

Besides being fun, learning a practical skill, planning, creating, carrying out a final product of which one is proud, is extremely satisfying to the soul. As a bonus, brain research has shown that "using the hands opens up neurological pathways that would otherwise atrophy." And then there's the fact that kids immersed in the arts show improvement academically, socially, emotionally, not even taking into account that it makes one's life more enjoyable, worth living.

Yet, once again, we hear that another administration wants to cut the budget of the arts' programs—all the fun, calming things which help to keep us mentally sound in this often confusing, sometimes scary world which these "representatives" have helped to create.

JUMP ROPES

Early in the year we would braid our own jump ropes, using three different colors of thirteen-foot-long strands of nylon. Besides the obvious benefits of fun, exercise, pride, and a reduction in stress, there were the bonuses of crossing the midline and team-building (We worked in teams of three: the holder, the braider, and the person who occasionally pulled out a strand to keep the rope from twisting.).

We would jump rope whenever we needed a break from our routine, if we were getting a bit sluggish, upset…and between tests. Occasionally, some classes would ask for competitions (the last few minutes of the day), which was good motivation for getting cleaned up quickly. We would create enough categories to persuade most of the kids to participate: Most jumps without a miss, jumps in a minute, creative routine, improved, jumps on one foot. When we were done, we would coil them up and return them to our desk or to a shelf beside their number.

Unfortunately, the skeins of colorful strips of polyester fabric (remnants of slips) we used to braid our jump ropes are not available at this time, but perhaps you could use heavy cotton roving, strips of panty hose, or even plastic bags. Or you could source these nylon strips and become entrepreneurs.

My classes provided the last three presidents, first ladies, and once, the first children and first mother-in-law, with braided red, white, and blue jump ropes to keep them in shape for their very demanding jobs. We sent these along with good thoughts and notes of congratulations.

WEAVING

One can buy commercial cardboard looms or make them yourself. For K-3 kids we cut the cardboard for a full sheet cake (purchased at a cake decorator's supply) into quarters which of course yields four looms. For a class or small group project you may at times wish to use a half or full sheet.

Make a mark every half inch (on both ends of the loom). You may cut a slot, or make a v-shaped notch with an x-acto blade, serrated knife, or you can save valuable time by purchasing a "pig's ear notcher" (available at a vet supply or some feed stores) which does the job much quicker and nicer, and is an interesting conversation piece.

The construction process can stop here, or you can add a ¾" dowel the width of the loom, 1 inch from the ends. This raises the warp, which makes it much easier, thus more enjoyable for the young weaver.

Instructions for warping the loom and projects can be found online.

If the kids (or you) enjoy weaving, you might also try straw weaving, card weaving, finger weaving, or weaving on an inkle loom.

KNITTING

One of my favorite times of the week was Friday afternoon, not because we would soon be getting a well-deserved break but because this was when my good friend, colleague, and master knitter would be joining us. Miss Mary Martin enriched our lives with fun, practical lessons such as sign language, but most of the children would remember her for her knitting instruction. This was the one day that my (present and former) students knew that, barring an emergency, they would not be able to visit during lunch hour as Miss Mary and I might be discussing a child, something which had transpired in our classroom, or anything which she needed to be aware of. Miss Mary would then make any repairs which the novice knitters required, missed stitches, tangled messes, and other mysteries well beyond my knowledge. The projects would be ready for the last hour when, if they had completed their assignments for the week, the kids could resume work on their scarves, felted cell phone cases, balls, and animals.

Some chose to sit by themselves, others preferred working with a partner, many enjoyed a group situation in a knitting circle on the carpet. Miss Mary recently helped me recall the visual of the "contortionist" who somehow managed to squeeze her highly flexible body into a minimal, empty space in a bookcase.

Those who were not enamored with knitting would be excused, AFTER they completed at least two rows of their project and a row on our "chemo cap," which we would donate to a local organization unless we were aware of a particular child who could benefit. After completing this requirement, they could choose to play an (educational) game, or read or write for enjoyment. Because Miss Mary was a certificated teacher, I was often able to work one-on-one with a child, listen to a problem, give an individual oral (untimed) math fact test, tutor, maybe have a necessary or elective conversation outside, provided I had completed my two rows. I *did not* receive special treatment. It was a perfect way to end the week. For a while, we were able to forget about academics, have an opportunity to talk, get to know each other better, have a bit of fun, and leave for the weekend relaxed and happy, with good thoughts about school and life.

It became necessary to limit this short period to student instruction as parents and other visitors were becoming interested in learning to knit, hoping for a refresher course, maybe a few pointers, a repair, or a quick fix. Miss Mary was nice enough to work with them when possible. She informed them of free classes at the library, and I promoted another free resource…their children could teach them everything that they'd learned in class, which could lead to some good conversations, a shared interest, and quality time. We were also noticing a great influx of auxiliary staff dropping by during this time, occupational therapists, resource specialists, psychologists, autism and other consultants, ostensibly to observe. Soon they were bringing their paper work, hanging out, chillin' in the calm, friendly, homey environment.

If you are interested, I bet you can find, on a knitting website, blog, at a local knitting get-together, or yarn shop, a passionate knitter who would just love to pass on their obsession, help teach you and your children how to knit, a life-long, fun, practical skill which just might help your student focus, lower their anxiety, elevate their mood, and conceivably super-size their self-esteem and confidence.

A special education teacher might tell you that knitting is beneficial because it uses "two-handed, bilateral, cross-body hand motions." For the joyful child, just seeing the beautiful object they have created, with their own hands, works for them.

Steven, a child diagnosed with autism, was fascinated with knitting, and soon became adept at making high-quality scarves. He and I made a verbal contract which basically said that if he maintained his "good practices" and completed all of his assignments for the week, I would buy him a couple skeins of yarn in his choice of hues. His first scarf was a solid color, his second, variegated camouflage, and then he would progress to producing professional-looking works of art in the colors of each of his favorite sports teams. I'd like to believe that knitting played a small part in boosting Steven's confidence, and contributed, if only a tiny sliver, to making him the beautiful person that he is today.

Robert had completed the required section of the BIG TEST. His options were to read, draw, or sit quietly without disturbing his neighbors. Rob chose instead to knit. Lacking his supplies, he attempted, unsuccessfully, to harvest some thread from the frayed hem of his shorts. It was then that he noticed a loose thread on his knit shirt, and gave it a little tug. He kept urging it, and the cooperative thread got progressively longer. Rob located one of his "testing" pencils and began to "cast on." Picking up a second pencil, he commenced to knit. An "avid" knitter knits at every opportunity.

Donald hunkered down, and refused to knit. If his friends found out that he was knitting, "he'd be toast," he informed me. Overhearing the conversation, Miss Mary Martin called him over and told him, "You know, Donald, knitting can get kind of violent!" *"IT CAN?"* "Oh yes, it sure can!" Miss Mary promised. "Come over here, let me show you." The little rhyme which the class had learned to remember the knit stitch, "Under the fence, catch the sheep, back it comes, and off it leaps," suddenly became, "POKE 'EM, TIE 'EM UP, YANK 'EM BACK, AND KNOCK 'EM OFF!" *"OH, I CAN DO THAT!"* an excited Donald announced! **HE COULD, and HE DID!**

ANTOINE

Antoine, over the protests of our administrator, came to our classroom as a "referral" from a friend of mine, a concerned person on the staff at his former school. Antoine was scheduled to be expelled from our school district. I am not in any way excusing or condoning what he did, but it was possible that he, like many children (and adults), was crying out for help. Antoine may have literally been trying to send smoke signals to anyone who would listen, as nothing else appeared to be working for him. I was willing to give Antoine a second chance in a new environment where he was not known, in his own words, as a "bad boy."

Fortunately, I knew in advance (which is not always the case) that Antoine would be joining us, and more rare, when he would be coming. To his advantage, he would be here on knitting day. I had time to familiarize Miss Mary Martin, our instructor, with his story, and we were able to discuss strategies.

After I introduced him to the class, I gave the other students independent work so I could acquaint Antoine with our basic rules. I informed him that this was his lucky day, as we would be spending the remainder of the day knitting. He could use my knitting needles today, but before our next session he would need to make his own.

Soon Miss Mary called me back, and whispered, just loud enough for me (and Antoine) to hear, "Mr. A, this is one of the best knitters I have ever worked with!" (which was not an exaggeration). Antoine sat up straighter than I thought possible, just short of levitating above his seat. "I had a feeling that he would be," I told her, "based on all of the things that I heard from my friend Mrs. B (the person who had "referred" him)." *"You know Mrs. B?"* he asked (obviously pleasantly surprised). "Oh yes," I said. "Mrs. B is a good friend of mine, and she will want to hear how you're doing. I'll send the first letter, and after that, it's up to you to keep her informed." Antoine left for the weekend with posture that would please a West Point cadet, and a huge smile.

The first recess on Monday, I took Antoine to visit some of my favorite people, the secretaries, the kindergarten teachers, and of course, the custodian. I introduced Antoine and informed them how lucky we were that he was at our school. In the hallway, Antoine (failing to hide a grin) asked, *"Mr. A, How many people are you going to tell about me?"* "Antoine, I'D TELL THE WHOLE WORLD IF I COULD!"

One wouldn't know by looking at his test results (He had scored in the FIRST PERCENTILE across the board on previous STANDARDIZED TESTS), but Antoine was (is) a "math whiz," and he soon became popular with those kids needing help. Antoine was now reminding the kids, *"Sit up you guys and listen to the teacher!"* Children will live up to your expectations. If you label them, treat them as a failure, they will often prove you right. If you show them respect, have realistic expectations, they will often make you proud.

When we got the test results for the BIG TEST, it was no surprise to me that Antoine scored in the ADVANCED range in Math! His reading/language arts score was in the PROFICIENT range! "*We knew he could do it!*" stated the current and former administrators when they saw what Antoine had achieved. Yes, WE did.

Antoine's reward for his hard work, besides a nice warm feeling inside for a job well-done, was that he earned the privilege of helping in the "special needs" class next door, and was able to help out other times in the K class. Antoine found out what it meant to be a SUPER STAR. He saw the looks on the faces of those five and six-year-olds when he entered their room and they were told by their teacher that this child was here to help them today, THIS BIG THIRD-GRADER, IN MY CLASS, AND HE'S HERE TO HELP ME!

Some of the easiest kids to work with are the "incorrigibles" with whom you take the time to listen, get to know. It's so much easier to "turn them around" when they are young and haven't yet been devoured and forgotten by society.

"It is easier to build strong children than to repair broken men."
—Frederick Douglass.

22 THE TEAM

PARENTS

Parents are a lot like you and me, you may even be one. Parents want the same things you and I do. They want to be respected and listened to. With very few exceptions, they want the best for their child, their pride and joy. If you put yourself in their shoes, you might not think them pushy or a troublemaker when they ask, fight for something which they believe will benefit their child's welfare. You may have done that yourself, wish you'd done that, or will someday want to do it for your own child. In your career, you will have plenty of opportunities to show your empathy, to listen to the input of a concerned parent who is trying their best to do one of the toughest jobs in the world.

Face -To-Face (f2f)

Whenever I want to talk to a parent, or anyone, about an important subject, especially one of a personal nature, such as anything affecting a child's education, I prefer face-to-face communication. When one is having a conversation on the phone, communicating through letters, emails or texts, others can misinterpret your meaning, not take you seriously, or underestimate the degree of your concern or passion. When you are in close proximity to another and establishing eye contact, your facial expressions and body language give the listener a better gauge of your feelings, your interest in them and their child, and the situation. They have your full, undivided attention, and you have theirs. I want each parent to know, especially those that I see infrequently, that may not know me, that I care deeply about their child, and want the best for them.

If the parent is uncomfortable in a school environment, we must be sensitive to their feelings. If there is a history of conflict, at this school or another, any real or perceived insensitivity or differences, we need to "clear the air," and trust each other. Nine months flies by, and there is no time to waste. We have an important job, which is to do everything we can, with their support, to ensure their child has all of the tools, and has mastered all the skills necessary, to prepare them for a successful educational career.

PARENT CONFERENCES

Almost from the beginning I enjoyed parent conferences. It was a chance to meet the parents of my students, get to know them, gain their support, and glean information about their child which might help me to better understand them, possibly identify a better way to get through to them. I say "almost from the beginning" because my first year of teaching I totally blew it with my parents. I followed the district policy of sending out letters to the parents of children who were below grade level in any of the academic standards. I sent out the designated form for the 26 children in my class who had "deficiencies" in one or more of these areas. When the parents weren't thrilled to meet with me, I soon figured out why. How would you feel as a parent if the first communication you got from your child's teacher was an indictment (in the mail) that their child was not doing well? What a slap in the face!

Hopefully, before the first parent conference, you will have had an opportunity to meet each parent, whether it's during a home visit, a welcome back spaghetti feed, or at Back-To-School Night. Each time you meet with them, let them know that you appreciate (because you do) that they took the time to meet with you. Let them know that their child also appreciates and benefits from this meeting — they see that we are working together because THEIR EDUCATION IS SO IMPORTANT.

I begin each conference with at least one POSITIVE statement about their child. We're very fortunate to have ___ in our class, he/she adds so much, has such a great personality, is so attentive, concerned about others, always has something to add to our discussions, tries to do their best, something that you believe is true. I've frequently been asked by parents, usually jokingly, if we were talking about the same child, but they do appreciate your kind words and this will help get you started on the right foot.

Provide the parent(s) with ample opportunity to give their input. Is there anything that I should know about your child, his/her needs, situation, strengths/weaknesses, which will help me work with them this year? Do you have any concerns? They should now be ready to listen to what you have to say.

The main reason for this conference is to let the parents know (truthfully) the academic and social progress of their child. A beneficial report should include a list of all the skills taught at that grade level (hopefully the parents would be familiar with this because they had been given this list early on), where the child is expected to be at this point, where they are, what skills they've mastered, which ones they are working on, and the plan for how the school and home can ensure that they will be prepared for the next grade. A parent will sometimes question your evaluation, or claim that their child can do that particular skill at home. Don't get defensive or into a power struggle because then everyone has lost, especially the child. This is their baby, and they have probably observed the same thing that you have. Give them an opportunity to save face. Assure them that you will do everything you can to help their child succeed this year, and if that isn't enough you will seek input from others.

The remainder of the time should be spent on other parts of the equation, social development, anything which might be keeping the child from reaching their potential. This could include behavior problems, difficulties focusing (attention or vision), not making friends (If they didn't already have one, you've found them a friend by now), overly aggressive, not arriving to school on time. I can't imagine having a beneficial conference in less than a half-hour.

"No Shows" may not be a problem at your school, but I tell the kids (and the parents) that this is one of the most important days of the year, it is crucial that they come. I provide early morning slots, mostly afternoon times, and late afternoon, early evening conferences for those who can come at no other time. I don't know if it's applicable anymore, but when children were being bussed, we would make one day available when a district bus provided transportation for parents with this need.

I send out reminders the day before the scheduled day, and at dismissal time I would read a list of who will be coming that day, the following day, and the day after that (today, on deck, in the hole), along with their times so the kids will remind their parents.

I am also willing to meet elsewhere if a parent appears anxious or distrustful, somewhere more "safe," a church, restaurant or other public place... An additional leverage I utilized was to tell the kids that if the parents were unable to make it to the school, I would be happy to do a home visit, thinking erroneously that most kids/parents wouldn't like this option. "I USUALLY TRY TO SHOW UP AROUND DINNER TIME!" I told them.

"I HOPE YOU LIKE BEANS!" one child warned.

Parent conferences can be enjoyable, are often eye-opening, usually beneficial, sometimes memorable, and can lead to a supportive relationship. Meeting twice a school year, a total of one hour, for the benefit of a child is not too much to ask.

A NEIGHBOR ASKED

A neighbor asked if I would write a letter for her, "telling my grand-daughter that she should listen to her mother and me." I listened to her concerns, and told her that she already knew what she wanted and needed, to say. Tell her the TRUTH, and SPEAK FROM YOUR HEART.

"The idea is to write it so that people hear it and it slides through the brain and goes straight to the heart."
—Maya Angelou

Here's a parent's note that would work for me:

A PARENT'S OATH

You are more precious to me than you can possibly imagine. You are as close as I've come to heaven on earth. You are smart, talented, and have a beautiful spirit. I love you, and admire you.

You are unique. There has never been and will never be another person exactly like you. I will not compare you to, or expect you to be like anyone else.

I vow to listen to you. If you have a question, I hope you will ask me. If something is bothering you or if you are worried about something, I hope that you will talk with me.

If you have a problem, I'll do my best to help you. If I can't, we'll find someone who can.

If you disagree with something I or anyone else says or does, it's all right, let's discuss it.

I will do anything to protect you from dangers, bullying, and unfair treatment. I will defend you against anyone.

If you do something wrong, I will forgive you; we all make mistakes. I, too, am human, so when I make a mistake, say the wrong thing, or get mad, please forgive me. I would never hurt you on purpose.

I will give you the best advice I know, try to put you on the right path, but will respect your right to be the person you are meant to be. I will make every effort not to discourage your hopes and dreams or impose mine on you.

Please talk to me, share with me. I want to hear everything you have to say. Give me the chance to show you all the love I have for you. You are the greatest joy of my life.

LET'S HEAR IT FOR THE AIDES

LET'S HEAR IT FOR THE AIDES, our unsung heroes who don't always get the credit they deserve. When I was a novice teacher, overwhelmed by the 31 individuals LOOKING AT ME, I was convinced that being an aide was the perfect job. You get to help kids, usually one-to-one, without ultimate responsibility, don't have to put up with all the "bureaucracy," and get to be "the good guy." Unfortunately, it was difficult enough trying to survive on a beginning teacher's salary let alone what they were paying the aides.

My introduction to these angels was at my first school, where they were a vital factor in a very successful reading program. I was fortunate through the years to have aides who not only provided essential academic support for the kids but were a joy to work with and exceptionally creative!

While I was giving large group instruction, a former, quite artistic aide was constructing pen, ink, and watercolor "balloon letters" for a bulletin board awards chart. Another day, with oil pastels, she drew pies and cakes (after an artist we were studying), for what would later become letters for an ARTIST OF THE MONTH board.

Another aide suggested the idea for one of our most popular projects ever, a science experiment (a prelude to our ceramics unit) which showed us what happened to different materials when placed in a kiln. We would first create clay pinch pots, about 3 inches in diameter, inscribed with the child's number, and then place the non-toxic object we chose in the pot. This would require two identical objects, one for the "before," and one to be sacrificed for the "after." A chart was constructed which listed the objects, a prediction of what we thought might happen to the object, and later what actually happened to the object when we put it in our school kiln at close to 2,000 degrees.

We made sure that a variety of materials was represented: candy (sugar), leather, coins (various metals), pencils (wood, graphite, metal), erasers, and dog biscuits. An example I treasure is one which we produced in honor of a child who left prior to our experiment. The Cheetos, Crunchy not Flamin' Hot, were chosen since the former student and I often joked about our love of this orange, highly-processed "snack," with little if any nutritional value. When subjected to the extreme heat, this junk food left a virtual physiognomy, one correctly placed eye, nose, a sad, down-turned mouth, and a suspended tear, seemingly portraying the child we all missed.

One of the last aides I worked with would interpret my lessons into visual representations, graphic organizers, breaking down the steps into more easily understood lessons for the child with autism whom she shadowed

All of these aides enriched my life, as well as those of my students, and were among the best teachers, and people, that I have known.

PRINCIPALS AND PRINCIPLES

I did not agree with all of the principals at the school sites, but I did learn something from each and every one of them. One highly-regarded administrator not only seemingly knew every one of his 400 students, the parents, and siblings, but was also familiar with their strengths, weaknesses, and triggers. This proved to be an invaluable tool in my career.

From a master, I learned the art of interrogation, of obtaining information quickly, reading a child's face and body gestures.

"Someone claiming to be your friend told me that it was YOU that ___."   "*No, it was her! It was ___!*"   OR   "Did you hit ___?"   "*No way, it wasn't me!*"   "I heard you hit her THREE times."   "*Who told you that? I only hit her twice!*"

I learned from numerous principals that if one has their favorites, their BFFs, and these favorites receive benefits from this relationship, special treatment, the morale of the staff will suffer. The irony is that even the "privileged group" will not have much respect for this kind of administrator.

As is common in other arenas, there are those who believe that "making nice," pretending that all is good, and that appearances, creating one's own reality, are more important than what is actually happening.

Perhaps it is because I've always been a dreamer that I presume that one of the principal's primary duties should be asking teachers, WHAT CAN I DO TO HELP YOU perform your crucial job of teaching all of your students? What materials, training do you need? What support, academically and emotionally, do your kids need? If one is struggling, challenged in an area, be it classroom management or effective teaching methods, it should be the administrator's job to recognize, and address the deficiency, the need, and to find a mentor to help, be it herself/himself, another staff member, or an outside qualified source. Too often principals skip this step, and instead spend extensive wasted time and energy trying to get rid of an individual rather than making an effort to help them.

A wise administrator will listen to input from teachers, other staff members, parents, and members of the community, not to mention our astute children. He/She may want to enlist a team of designated representatives from each class, including the primary grades, to solve, with simple solutions, your persistent problems.

If a principal should ever forget why they chose this profession, why they were hired, I offer a temporary reminder which some may wish to use as a model for creating a pledge to themselves, their teachers, and the children who rely on them. They might want to read it occasionally to get themselves in the right state of mind to rededicate their efforts to a vital job.

A PRINCIPAL'S OATH

I am here for one reason and one reason only, our students. I have been given the opportunity and the great responsibility to affect the lives of hundreds of children.

I vow that I shall do everything in my power to see that each of them receives the best, well-rounded education possible, in a safe, positive environment.

I will be the facilitator of a team which works together for the benefit of all our students. I will set an example by LISTENING and VALUING the input of our teachers and other staff members, the students, their parents, and members of the community. Each of us has an essential piece to contribute.

Every member of our team is crucial. If any of them is struggling, having a problem, needs help, I will listen and offer assistance or find someone who can.

Everything one hears about our school is true. What you see and feel when you visit our campus is evident and undeniable. We are proud of our entire team, and are successful because we all care and are working towards a common goal, the success of every child.

HIRING A TEACHER

If you find yourself faced with the all-important responsibility of hiring a teacher, you may want to consider some of the following guidelines. These could also be utilized as part of a self-check list to determine if one has chosen the appropriate profession. I am aware that the school, the district, and the teachers' union often have different, conflicting ideas, demands, some of which are valid, and others which could ultimately be detrimental to the education of the children.

Once the applicants have been narrowed down by whatever criteria is utilized, a panel composed of representatives from the following: the principal, a teacher from the segment where the teacher would be placed (ideally one that would be working with the selected teacher), a parent, an auxiliary staff member, and possibly a member of the community, might want to consider posing some of the following questions:

WHY DID YOU GET INTO TEACHING?

If the response is a variant of one of the following, or has nothing to do with liking, or wanting to help children, you might want to look elsewhere:
• Thought that you would do this until you found something else (possibly a job which paid more)
• You're into power
• The long vacations
• Sounded like an easy job

DO YOU HAVE A PROBLEM WITH, WOULD YOU FEEL UNCOMFORTABLE WORKING WITH:
• A child of a certain race, ethnic group, or religion?
• A child with a learning, physical, mental, or emotional challenge?

ARE YOU WILLING TO WORK, COLLABORATE WITH OTHERS (teachers, other staff, parents, and members of the community)?

WHAT EXPERIENCES DO YOU HAVE WORKING WITH CHILDREN, INCLUDING CHILDREN WITH CHALLENGES? Be specific.

To test their writing skills and values, you might ask them to compose a rough draft of something akin to "A Teacher's Oath" (which follows this section), where they would express what they would pledge to do for our children.

The last part of the screening process would be a demonstration lesson in which the applicant is observed instructing a class, as a substitute or with the classroom teacher present, hopefully in the segment where the vacancy is. The logistics could be worked out for this most important tool.

Of course, one's intuition, vibes, impression about the applicant's character, warmth, abilities, as well as their references, should contribute greatly to the equation.

A TEACHER'S OATH

You, my students, are the reason I got into teaching. You are my inspiration for coming to school each day.

I vow to do all that I can, using all resources available, to ensure that you and every child in my class has a superior well-rounded education.

I pledge that you will be exposed to the arts, sciences, physical education, and the latest technology as you are becoming proficient in reading, math, and the language arts.

I will work with the other teachers, share my talents, strengths, ideas, and projects so that you and all students will benefit from our combined knowledge.

I will provide a safe, positive environment within the classroom, without put-downs or sarcasm so that you feel free to express your thoughts.

I will make time to listen to your ideas and concerns whether they are school-related or based elsewhere.

I will defend you against anyone.

I care about each of you; I will treat you fairly, and not show favoritism.

I will never forget how fortunate I am to be able to work with children. I will do everything in my power to be a champion, an advocate for you, the future leaders of our society.

ACTUAL STATEMENTS BY EDUCATORS

We've all said hurtful things to kids. We were shocked at what we said and vowed to not repeat our blunders. We got into the education field because we care about kids, and our occasional indiscretion is usually said out of frustration, not malice. Should this prove to be otherwise, become the norm, if you're not in it for the children, do EVERYONE a favor and get some help, or find another career.

The following statements were made by individuals who could fall into the latter category:

"You've got as much brains as a soda cracker."

"It's sink or swim in my class."

(Yelling) "Shut up, C! I said shut up! Just shut up, shut up, C!"

"I hate first-graders. They don't listen, and they're always talking."

"You, sit in that corner, and you, in that one. You can stay there all year for all I care. I just don't want to hear you!"

"I hope you don't expect much from ___. His mother's a ___, and his father's a ___!"

"Kids are nothing but trouble. If you've been teaching for as long as I have, you'd know what I was talking about."

"You are so dumb. You'll never amount to anything." (I have heard from so many people that this was said to them, their sibling, a friend, or classmate.)

The one I heard the most often, sometimes in words, more often in actions, was "I DON'T WORK WITH THOSE KIDS"—covering everything from the color of their skin, to learning, behavioral, physical or emotional challenges, including "special needs" kids.

23 STIGMAS

"Dear Mr. Anderson, we were playing with your brain and cannot put it together again."

Fortunately, these two students were referring to a model of the brain which they had borrowed.

We are all born with DIFFERENT brains, not GOOD or BAD brains. It's almost as if someone planned it that way so that all of the skills necessary for the plethora of jobs needed in our society would be provided for.

Unfortunately, in our schools, and in our society, we continue to stigmatize certain types of brains. The child who can sit quietly in an uncomfortable seat and listen to an adult talking at them for six hours, five days a week, without complaining, getting bored or restless, has been blessed, according to many, with the desired type of brain. If one was born with the type of brain which determined that they could be labeled with some type of "disorder" or "syndrome," **say** A.D.D., dyslexia, or Asperger's Syndrome, there might be a painful stigma attached.

A.D.D.

A.D.D., I'm pretty sure, means ATTENTION DEFICIT DISORDER, not A DEATH DIAGNOSIS. When I would tell a parent at a conference that their child was having some difficulties "focusing," or "being attentive," they might initially react by blaming the other side of the family, and progress to, "Oh, no, you don't mean that he/she has (THE DREADED) A.D.D.!"

"This is just an observation," I would tell them. We should monitor the times when they are inattentive. Is it when they are reading something which they don't find interesting, when someone is lecturing? Is it much of the time? The parent may have already observed this, or heard it from another teacher, they may know of someone in the family with similar tendencies. I would occasionally hear something similar to, "I bet you don't know anyone who has A.D.D.!" "*I probably do*," I tell them, "and so do many of my intelligent and creative friends."

I suggest that they might want to make an appointment with their child's pediatrician, and with an optometrist to make sure that it is not something visual. Has their child had a recent physical, been checked for food allergies? Do they eat foods which contain a lot of sugar or white flour? Are they getting plenty of sleep, not spending too much time staring at screens or hooked up to electronic devices? Are they getting enough exercise? They might want to take up a sport, meditation, yoga, tai chi, or a martial art.

The conversation may turn to the topic of medication. I listen to their concerns, and tell them my opinion, that this should be the last resort. Many kids who are medicated should not be, and some that aren't could be. Girls are, I believe, under-diagnosed. Find a doctor that you trust. If the situation is not addressed, many will later resort to SELF-DIAGNOSIS and SELF-MEDICATION, which doesn't always work out well!

If something is diagnosed, it is important to make it clear to the child that THIS DOES NOT MEAN THAT THEY ARE NOT SMART. It is important to reinforce this even if nothing is diagnosed when they are being barraged by tests.

Ethan, a child with classic A.D.H.D. (A.D.D. with hyperactivity) symptoms was continuously in motion, could not relax, was unable to focus. His ability to read was impaired.

One memorable day, Ethan entered the classroom, sat down quietly, was attentive, focused, and during oral reading, his classmates and I heard him read fluently for the first time. Later in the day, we marveled as he sat calmly and untangled a huge mass of yarn on which the rest of us had given up. I called his mom to inform her of the miraculous transformation, and to ask what had transpired since we talked at our conference. Ethan's pediatrician had diagnosed him with A.D.H.D., recommended medication, and his mom had agreed to give it a try. A couple weeks later, Ethan entered the class, fidgety, incapable of settling down, and we soon learned, was unable to read. I again called his mom. Kids had been teasing him (one child, with similar challenges), so she decided to take Ethan off the meds. And that's how things remained for the rest of the year.

ADULT A.D.D.

A "celebrity" being interviewed by a talk show host appeared to be devastated and in deep pain. I was curious as to the cause of her suffering, a death in her family, the diagnosis of a chronic disease. We learn that she was recently diagnosed with "Adult A.D.D." I attempted, unsuccessfully, to contact her, to console her that her A.D.D., rather than a roadblock, was possibly a factor in her success. This is the same brain which perpetually gifts her with the awesome ideas which contribute to the creative, impressive person that she is, the reason she was invited to appear on this show, why people are interested in hearing her story.

I've been cognizant of the effects of my A.D.D. for most of my life. Yes, it is often difficult to focus, and when your mind doesn't shut off easily, one doesn't always get a good night's sleep (Having a notebook and pencil nearby to transcribe my thoughts, rather than thinking about them all night, helps me.) but I wouldn't give up my A.D.D. for the world…the pleasure, the high I receive from the zillions of ideas racing through my head is priceless. I don't remember ever being bored!

DYSLEXIA

Our education system, our society, fails far too many individuals, by some an estimated 10 to 20 percent of our population. When I made the decision to quit teaching to become a caregiver for a family member, I began to give some thought to whether I would eventually return to teaching. Perhaps I would rent a small building, and provide free tutoring to those in need. I even approached a motorcycle club, thinking that perhaps I could use their clubhouse as a home base.

The reality is that many of the adults with (severe) reading challenges that I had hoped to help are not always receptive. Whether they don't want people to know of their "disability" because they are embarrassed that others might think them less intelligent, due to a perceived societal stigma, they may have had such a bad experience as a child that they were not willing to go through more pain, or they rationalized that they made it this far and could survive the rest of their life without additional reading skills, they usually pass on the offer.

I am asked by some parents (or I volunteer) to diagnose their child. If the prognosis suggests dyslexia, I find that the STIGMA in our society is often more powerful than the HOPE of helping their child. Many choose to disregard, deny, or bury the diagnosis. Perhaps the parent also had this challenge and wants to protect their child from the false hopes that they experienced, they don't want their friends, neighbors, or the school to know and label their child, or because of the immense amount of work that they assume it would entail, MOST will not follow through with my recommendations.

If there is a quick fix, if I can somehow "cure" them without anyone knowing, they are amenable. To many, anything less is not worth exploring. Things which I would just do without anyone's knowledge when I was teaching, are not always plausible outside the classroom.

We're stigmatizing so many people for the kind of brain they were born with. There are millions of gifted, talented, creative people with similar challenges, architects, artists, actors, dancers, CEOs... Hopefully (SOON) there will come a time when we decide that ENOUGH IS ENOUGH, and take the time, the energy, to teach reading with alternative programs for those who are not learning by traditional methods. We should supplement our reading adoptions with other proven programs, including all available technology, and enlist the help of volunteers, grandmothers (and grandfathers), neighbors, college students, and employees loaned from corporations.

ASPERGER'S SYNDROME

Many think of SILICON VALLEY when they hear the term "ASPERGER'S SYNDROME" (the true revenge of the nerds?), but this diagnosis is shared with brilliant, productive people from all walks of life.

HARRY

When the concerned, supportive parents of Harry received the diagnosis of Asperger's Syndrome, on the high-functioning end of the autistic spectrum, they would make the huge decision to travel a great distance to seek the services of a respected research center. Somehow, he found his way into our classroom, and quickly found his way into our hearts. There were some issues initially. I confess to being flummoxed, unsure what to do.

From day one, Harry was treated just like any other child. Why wouldn't he be? He was as attentive as any student I've ever had. He would study my facial expressions, body gestures, listen to my every word. No matter the academic subject, Harry was a model student. What more could a teacher ask for? Like most people I know, he did have some "special" needs. He looked to his teacher and other adults for cues of appropriate behavior, which he gradually assimilated. He did take what I and others said quite literally so it was necessary to adjust my sense of humor, which not many fully appreciate anyway.

My friend, colleague, and class knitting instructor, Miss Mary Martin, recalled Harry. "Not only did he like knitting, and want to practice every chance he got, he wanted to learn everything there was to know. When he saw my check list— knit, purl, bind off, cast on, increase, decrease— he asked what I was doing. I explained that I would check off what he already knew, and when he could do everything on the list, that he would know as much as I did about knitting. That did it! This was his new challenge, his new goal, and it did not take him long to achieve it. As far as I know, the only one who was troubled by Harry's new skill was his good friend D. 'All Harry wants to do is knit," he complained.

Oh, the issues, you may be thinking. Actually, the issues were all mine. You see, Harry was as polite a child as had ever walked into a classroom, a true Southern gentleman. When called upon, HE WOULD STAND, and with respect that floored me, would address me as SIR. Just BLEW MY MIND! That's 60s or 70s talk, which translates as "to affect with intense emotion, such as amazement... or shock." The children were oblivious to my concern, and soon adopted the practice of standing when they spoke. The SIR never caught on.

At the last of many conferences, his parents asked me what would happen to him next year. "That is totally up to you," I answered. "Harry is an amazing kid who should fit in anywhere as long as he has a teacher who is sensitive to his needs. He requires more practice on social cues, and some additional 'social stories' on trust, but for Harry, the sky's the limit!" We would miss Harry. Trusting my assessment, the family decided to make the long journey home, where I'm confident Harry is still doing wonderful things.

ADRIANA

Some might find Adriana more challenging. Sharp, creative, artistic and FEISTY, Adriana enjoyed testing the boundaries. I am fond of challenges, and I like *feisty*! Most of my friends would probably consider me "feisty." Adriana made great strides that year, academically and socially, including managing her filters. She and other "Aspies" (their word) often have difficulties controlling what comes out of their mouths, a problem many of us non-Aspies share. Adriana was a character, and I enjoyed her immensely.

Several years later, Adriana would drop off a decorated, framed letter. These letters from the children and parents would often be what kept me going. Adriana offered a few compliments, which I knew were sincere because, as those who are familiar with children and adults with Asperger's know, THEY TELL (what they perceive to be) THE TRUTH! Adriana went on to list what she enjoyed about third grade, the art, any creative project. Her favorite part of the year, like many of the other children I later heard from, had been OUTDOOR EDUCATION, specifically our field trip to a working ranch. We prepared for the trip by learning about local history, and that day we dressed as we would have a hundred years ago. Our whole day was spent OUTSIDE in the fresh air, gardening, making candles, corn husk dolls, biscuits and butter from scratch, and a wooden stool or tool box. In between stations, we would play period games like bean bag toss or propelling a hoop with a stick. We found time to eat/share the simple lunches we had brought in our basket, can, or handkerchief. For one entire day, all was simple, STRESS-FREE, and "copacetic."

Adriana had many gifts and talents. One, of which she was especially proud, was her ability to braid a jump rope (a good exercise for crossing the mid-line) quickly and tightly. She wondered if her record for braiding a 13-foot jump rope in 5 ½ minutes still stood. That will be a hard one to break, Adriana!

Some keys to working with ANY child with ANY issue are: EARLY INTERVENTION, knowledge, and understanding. A bit of PATIENCE is also beneficial.

Maybe we, as educators, could lead the movement to rid these "disorders" of the stigmas they now engender, by pledging to become knowledgeable about the needs of these children, giving them the respect that we bestow upon all of our children, and doing whatever necessary to help them reach their potential, whether this necessitates providing services at any early age to aid their social development or utilizing an alternative method of teaching reading. Help ALL children see that this does not mean that they are not smart. They ALL have gifts, talents, strengths, that should be utilized to their fullest advantage and shared with the world. We might also consider giving these "challenges" more positive names, maybe dropping the labels "DISORDERS" AND "SYNDROMES."

24 A FEW OF MY STUDENTS

RUBY

One morning I got the word that I would be getting a new student from out of town whose father had just passed away. When she arrived with her mom, I offered my sincere condolences, and told her that if she ever wanted to talk, with me or the kids, we were available. Mother and daughter agreed that she wanted and needed to talk but she wasn't sure what to say. From personal experience, I was aware that if one does not talk to someone about death, especially that of a close friend or relative, issues such as confusion and anxiety might surface later.

I decided to skip the story we were scheduled to read that morning, and instead chose one about a girl who was missing her good friend who had moved away. After we read and discussed the story, I told the kids that we would be writing poems, using one of the following titles: If It Weren't For You, I Will Always Remember, I Will Miss, or something similar which had to do with loss. Since I was interested primarily in their thoughts (and the therapeutic value), we would be scaffolding (with which they were familiar), where each of the ten or so lines begins with the same words as the title. Yes, they could write about a family member. A friend would certainly be appropriate. A pet, sure. Divorce? If you want to. I would help with spelling, but this time I was more concerned with their ideas, I told them.

As we were finishing up our rough drafts, a parent came through the door with an early dismissal note for his son. I asked if he could possibly wait a couple minutes to allow his son to finish his poem. The dad walked over to the child's desk and they hugged. I offered the father a chair and he sat down and read the poem his son wrote. This seemingly tough, stoic character was idolized by many of the kids in the neighborhood because of his pan-head, vintage Harley. The person on the inside got the better of him, and the tears started to flow. Only he would know which line did it, which of the things about his father the son would miss, or maybe it was just the "Love, Your son ___." Our principal chose this time to visit, and seeing me standing there next to a father and son in tears, she rolled her eyes and gave me one of those familiar "WHAT DID YOU DO THIS TIME?" looks. I located a box of tissues, and asked the father if he would like to go outside for some "fresh air." He asked if he could take the poem with him, so I asked the principal if she would be able to make a copy. She returned shortly, and for a person not known for displaying her emotions, her eyes were curiously wet and red-rimmed.

Many of the students chose to read and explain their poems, including our new student. Soon there wasn't a dry eye in the room.

NATHANIEL KING

One never knows what a student will take from your class, what will inspire them, upset them, what they will remember. Take the case of Nathaniel King.

When gifts and talents were handed out, Nat was one of those children who had the audacity, and the foresight, to sneak back into the line over and over again. Whatever was asked of him, he would consistently exceed one's expectations.

I recall a particular school art contest, which must have had a patriotic theme because my second-grade students were drawing flags. Most of the kids drew two-dimensional banners, appropriate for a seven-year old. Nat's, in contrast, appeared to be rippling in a stiff breeze.

When I ran into Nathaniel about a decade later at a local record store (which was then selling CDs), I was eager to hear the direction his life had taken. He informed me that he was attending a university, and was considering a major in speech pathology, because nobody (including me) had helped his classmate and friend with his speech "impediment."

Nathaniel was right. We had received no training in screening for speech challenges. When I discussed this child with my colleagues, they seemed to be in the same boat as me. "Isn't he cute?" they asked. "Eventually, he will grow out of it," they assured me. Evidently, he hadn't.

Another lesson we should include in our teacher training… screening for proper speech development.

I WILL NOT WASTE THIS BRAIN

Wade, an obviously bright child, had a history of refusing to do any work. He continued this noncompliance in my classroom. Wade was not otherwise disruptive, disobedient, defiant, or oppositional. After exhausting almost every trick in my arsenal, I asked him to stay in during a recess. I shook my head in exasperation, told him to get something to write with, provided him with a piece of paper, and dictated the following letter:

Dear Mom, Dad, (The Principal), and Mr. Anderson,
I promise that from this day on, I will no longer waste this magnificent brain of mine!
Love, Wade

"Do I have to go to the principal?"   "No," I answered.
"Are you going to call my parents?"   "No," I responded.
"What's going to happen?"   I thought.

"Wade, I don't understand why you are not working. You are obviously smart, and otherwise well-behaved. I'm going to give you one last chance. I will keep this letter in your file in case we ever need it."

Fortunately, for whatever reason, Wade started working the next day, and we had no further problems!

His brother, who would end up in my room the next school year, was pleased to assume the role of the "good child," and would be super-compliant each of the 180+ days!

MONICA

Monica, a third grader, had been receiving services from the speech therapist since pre-school. I was pretty sure that she could read, but it was difficult to tell because she would stutter whenever asked to read out loud.

I frequently vacationed along the coast, where I sometimes found "fossils" on the beach. I told Monica about this, and that whenever I held this particular fossilized shell (which was about 5 million years old) in the palm of my hand, I was able to relax. It was like magic!

I asked Monica if she wanted to try it out. While she was clutching the shell, she read the first complete sentence that I had heard her read in class. "Keep it," I told her, "And I'll listen to you again later in the day." At that reading, Monica was able to read two sentences without stuttering. Within the week, she was reading an entire paragraph!

A couple of weeks later Monica came to see me, quite upset. She told me that she had lost the fossil. I tried to reason with her that many people had probably possessed it before us, and that when *we* needed it, we somehow found it. "Now that *you* don't need it anymore, wouldn't it be nice if someone who *does* need it could find it?" I asked her. She nodded her head and smiled.

We soon got a visit from the speech therapist, questioning what was going on in this room.

A TALENT

Unlike many, I enjoy working with the "tougher" kids (my share or a bit more), those with "behavior" problems, those who have been mistreated, labeled from a young age, those that don't fit the "common mold." I thrive on problem solving, a good challenge, and hate to see anyone struggling. I find that these kids are often among the easiest to work with. As you already know, or will soon learn, those with conduct problems are usually crying out for help, hungry for someone to listen to their pleas. Once one realizes this, discovers what's tormenting them, cares enough to get them back on track, you just may have a loyal friend for life, and an eager worker once his/her strengths and hidden talents are revealed to them...and they see their value reflected in your eyes.

Arriving to my new teaching assignment, I was welcomed with warm greetings. I was also probed by almost all with the inquiry, *"Do you have a TALENT?"* "Well, I'm not bad at photography." *"No, Do you have a TALENT?"* "I'm fair at drawing," I tried again. Each would shake their head in frustration. It turned out that TALENT was the last name of a family attending the school. I checked my class list and was able to answer no, I did not. They confided, "Lucky you, that the two brothers are in other classes, as they've been TROUBLE ever since pre-school."

Within a week or so, "the worst brother" and his teacher acknowledged that they had a major personality conflict. I approached this teacher, explaining that I was sure she was quite capable of handling the situation, but IF she felt uncomfortable at some point, I would be willing to take him. After probably assessing my sincerity and sanity, she readily accepted. My only request was that she approach the principal and the child's parents to verify that they were amenable to the change.

The next day I told my third graders that we had the chance to make a difference in a person's life, to give a child a second chance, a new start. The children, being the great kids they were, responded positively, excited for the opportunity. "As long as it isn't __!" I was taken aback as that, of course, was the child who would be their new classmate. They went on and on, in detail, what Charles had done in pre-school, kindergarten, first and second grades. We could try, I proposed, to forgive him for what he did in the past, and if only in our classroom, let him start anew. The children reluctantly agreed to give it their best shot.

After our opening ritual the following day, I explained to the kids that they would be working independently on their Project Picture Books, and that I would be working until recess with Charles. If they had questions or got stuck they could whisper to their neighbor. I trusted them. Our new student arrived, accompanied by the principal. One of his classmates got him situated in his assigned desk and provided him with necessary materials while I spoke with my boss. "I, or someone, will check up on Charles every hour to see if he is behaving," she explained. "For each hour that he is *good* he will get a cookie. That's what he's used to."

I smiled. "No, he'll do what everyone else is doing because that is what is expected of him in this classroom. His reward will be that he gets to participate in learning, and projects which he might find fun. No cookies, but you're welcome to visit him or us at any time, as long as we are not testing. You *are* welcome to bring the *whole class* a treat whenever. As you are aware, counting me, there are 32 of us."

I invited Charles back to the table where I informed him that he would be creating a picture book, which the other students had been working on for the past week. I explained the requirements, and that he was lucky because this one time I would allow him to dictate (tell me) the story and I would write it down for him.

"I CAN'T DO THAT!" he announced. "Why not?" I asked. *"Because you won't let me write what I want to write about!"* "Try me," I challenged. "Write about something which is interesting to you, and try to communicate to me and everyone else what you want us to know, that's all writing is. So, what are you excited about,

Charles?" *AIRPLANES!*" he answered, smiling. "Me, too!" I added.

Soon we completed the twelve or so pages of the rough draft, after which he copied them in his own handwriting. "Now, Charles, remember what I told you these books were called?" *"Picture books,"* he replied. "Now it's time to illustrate, to draw, pictures for at least half of the pages," I told him. *"I CAN'T DRAW!"* he groaned. I handed him some markers with the instructions to sketch his pictures with pencil, and then outline them with the markers while I returned to work with the rest of the class. About half an hour later I heard, *"Mr. A, I'm finished!"* I examined his completed project, and asked him, "Are you KIND OF proud or REALLY proud of yourself?" *"REALLY PROUD!"* he proclaimed. I told him that we'd be making the title, dedication and About the Author pages another day. I directed the class to put their books away. I announced that we had a new author in the class, and that Charles would be reading his book after recess. *"WHAT?"* he said, attempting to hide a huge grin.

Upon returning to the classroom, I pretended not to notice as he ran to the "author's chair" which I had placed in front of the room. Charles, apparently pleased with himself, with his new status, proceeded to share his creation. Just in time to hear the final pages, and witness the standing ovation, the principal entered the room. Fortunately, one of the children noticed her pallor, and graciously offered her a chair.

Charles, a child who had been labeled since pre-school, would challenge me only once that year. Sauntering into the classroom one morning, he blurted out, *"I DON'T FEEL LIKE WORKING TODAY, SO I WON'T!"* The rest of the class woke up (finger snap) like that, and looked at me, waiting for my response. Perhaps it was the full moon, or the howling North wind, I too was a bit agitated that day, and I was not going to take any garbage from anyone!

"That's OK," I said, "No problem." *"Huh?"* he grunted. "There's a law which says that you have to be in school, but no law that says that you have to work!" "Clear everything out of your desk and stack it up over there on the shelf."

OK," he said. Charles smiled, looking around for approval, sure that he had won.

"When you've finished, sit in this chair," which I was placing in the back of the room. He immediately tried to relocate the chair near a table.

"No, we will be needing this table, please move the chair back where it was!" No way I was going to allow him to get comfortable. Still smiling, he looked around to make sure that he had the kids' attention. While the rest of us were writing in our journals, Charles got up and headed towards our library.

"Where are you going, Charles?" I asked him. *"I'm going to read."* "No, I said that you didn't have to work. That does not mean that you can read or do whatever you wish to do! Please return to your seat." He then tried to retrieve a pencil and a piece of paper.

"No, Charles." I inserted an unplanned (fun) origami project into our lesson. No work, but no projects either.

Halfway through the morning he proclaimed that he was ready to come back. "I am sure that we all heard you say that you didn't feel like working today. Charles, don't you think that the rest of us have days when we don't feel like working? What do you think my boss, your principal, would say if I walked into her office and told her that I didn't feel like working today?" *"She'd fire you!"* he laughed. "You might be right," I conceded. "I'll tell you what, you can ask the rest of the class what they think. They will be your jury." He did, and accepted their consequences. Charles would stay in his seat until lunch. He would be able to eat, and then would sit on the bench near the office where he would begin the work he failed to do in class. Whatever he did not finish he would complete at home. To the best of my memory, that was the last groaning and complaining we heard from him, and we sailed relatively smoothly through the rest of the year.

A Child's Plea   161

In the subsequent years of his elementary school career, Charles would try to convince his teachers to allow him to return to Room 10 (my classroom), often (for some reason) with success.

In fifth grade, upon discovering that he would be having a substitute, Charles hatched a plan. Here is the note which he assumed would do the job.

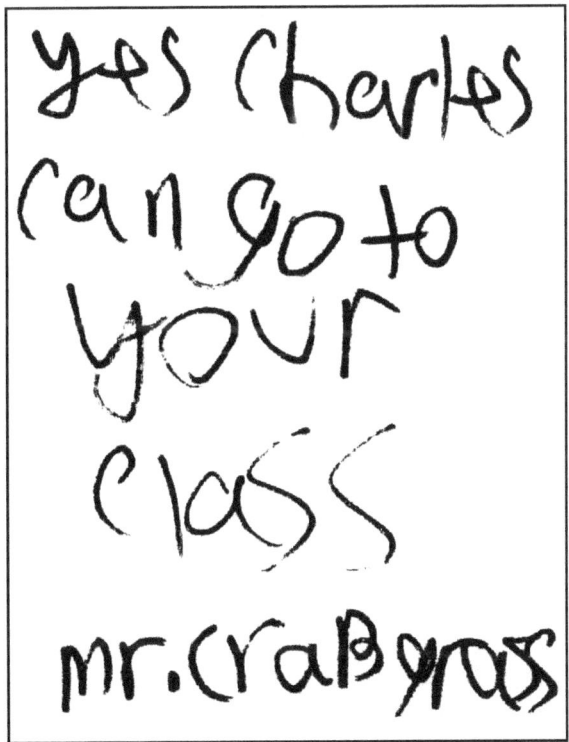

25 EVERY FOUR YEARS

Every four years, the children and I celebrated election time. Early in the school year we would begin collecting political posters, buttons, and brochures which we pinned on our ELECTION bulletin board. We would create election books (social science and handwriting) explaining our unique system, the requirements to run, political parties, their platforms, campaigning, touching on the electoral system so they could keep track the night of the election. We would make our own posters with ourselves as the candidate and make speeches about what we would do for the country if elected.

I would simplify an actual voting registration form which my students and those from the other participating classes had to fill out. The actual voting was done in our room (except the years when we were able to talk the county out of a few voting booths), one class at a time, on simple ballots with the name of the candidates alongside a box in which they would scribe their X. Kindergarteners had a similar ballot with a picture of each candidate. All were given an "I VOTED" sticker which they displayed proudly all day or until it fell off. Votes were counted by a team of students which varied depending on the school, and the winner was announced, just prior to departure time, by a representative from the oldest group.

Unfortunately, the strong divisions and rhetoric which currently exist make it more difficult to appreciate this process, this tradition, but hopefully this will one day change.

On the day following the national election we would compose and send individual letters congratulating the victor, along with a short bio of the sender and some profound recommendations.

We would send along hand-made jump ropes for the first family, to help maintain their health and physical stamina.

We were thrilled, and knew our voices had been heard, if we received a "personal" response from the most powerful person in the world!

In my view, a president's legacy begins its formation well before their first day in office. It is launched with their stated and observed morals, values, how they see and treat other people. If presidents had even a clue about the magnitude of influence they have on young, impressionable children, if they had genuine compassion for the welfare of our nation's greatest resource, they would reconsider the often-irresponsible discourse they throw around, seemingly without any regard to who their audience includes. Many of you would be SHOCKED were I to tell you what current and former students (elementary school age) have shared with me, what they learned from the person holding the highest elected office in our country, what they heard was ok, were encouraged, to feel, say, and do.

THE WHITE HOUSE
WASHINGTON

March 30, 2001

Dear Students:

Thank you for sending me the handmade red, white, and blue jump ropes. I am happy to see a sample of your work.

Mrs. Bush joins me in sending our best wishes.

Sincerely,

George W. Bush

26 MAPPING THE WORLD BY HEART

I attempted, unsuccessfully, to interest my colleagues in a geography program called "Mapping the World by Heart." The gist of this unit is that all students in grades 3-6 (3-8 if possible) follow a sequential course of study with the ultimate goal of being able to map out (ideally in freehand) the continents, countries, capitals, oceans, seas, major rivers and mountain ranges of the world.

Kids are interested in learning about other parts of the world, the people and their cultures, even if many adults are not. "Current events" are so much more meaningful if we know where they are taking place and something about the people involved.

27 ALL VARIETIES

I've worked with just about all "varieties" of children out there, from the affluent to those living in abject poverty, all races, the major religions, LGBTQ, and I have come to the grand conclusion that **KIDS ARE KIDS**. Contrary to what some rogue scientist or anyone else would have you believe, one race, one gender, is not superior, or inferior to another, in intelligence or any other metric. **ALL** children can thrive on an equal playing field.

28 PRIVILEGED

I became aware early on that I was being treated differently than some of my friends and classmates. Despite my mother's protestations (in jest, because of my hair and skin coloring) that I was switched at birth with a Native-American child, I entered this world as a Caucasian, a white person.

Firmly attached to my birth certificate was a GOLDEN TICKET which guaranteed certain privileges, advantages, benefits, not automatically assured those of other skin tones. Throughout my life, with relatively few exceptions, I've had the luxury of not having to even contemplate, let alone analyze the color of my skin, my racial background.

I credit the vast majority of our sentient population with the intelligence to recognize this reality. In order to promote positive change in our society, and our education system, we must acknowledge this well-established "most-favored" treatment and its inherent injustices.

PEOPLE **CAN** CHANGE

Before I was even situated in my new home, I had a surprise visit from a neighbor. This was not a social call, nor was he there representing the friendly neighborhood "welcome wagon." He was there as an individual, promising me that if I ever sold my house to a ___, (I will not repeat the slurs, but basically this encompassed anyone who did not look like he did), he would "hunt me down and kill me."

Remarkably, when he accepted my invitations to sit down with some of my friends, many of whom would fit into his categorizations, he was pleasant and got along with them quite well.

Our neighborhood is now enriched by people representing cultures from diverse parts of the world. If he were alive today, I'm pretty sure that this same person would accept these "newcomers" and enjoy their company. He would be comforted to know that they, too, take great pride in their property, just as he always did.

29 HISTORY MONTH

As would become increasingly more common, if not predictable, unfiltered words, emanating from somewhere other than my conscious mind, would escape my maw. I questioned less and less where they came from, and learned to quickly assess if the expression aligned with my principles, my beliefs.

A parent asked what I'd be doing for "History Month." I responded that I would be doing the same things I do EVERY SINGLE DAY of the school year. IN THIS CLASSROOM (of second and third-graders), we recognize the accomplishments of ALL individuals, celebrate heroes of ALL COLORS, GENDERS. In an age-appropriate way, we discuss our country's factual history, including injustices, and take opportunities to role play in a not too scary simulation so that the young children are able to, for instance, empathize with the disenfranchised, the marginalized. If I were "ANY-American," of either gender, I would be QUITE UPSET if I was allocated only a week, or even a month out of the year!

Most young children, at least those whom I've known, do not like to be singled out. They need to know that there are people WHO LOOK LIKE THEM teaching, represented in the books they read, the artists they study, the people they see on television, in the movies, and in leadership roles, and they want to be respected, judged for, WHO THEY ARE, not what they look like or their beliefs.

Most of my adult friends (I've finally figured out) feel much the same way. Many are tired of being patronized by their well-meaning friends. They consider themselves AMERICANS, and more important, HUMAN BEINGS, and want to be seen, thought of, and treated as such *every day of the year!*

30 A RIGHT OR A PRIVILEGE

One hears comments, arguments, and debates about whether education is a RIGHT or a PRIVILEGE. I maintain that it should be the right of **every** person to receive a quality, well-rounded education, but it is also essential that parents (and other members of society) believe and instill in their children, that the opportunity to attend school, to get an education, is a PRIVILEGE, A PRICELESS GIFT.

What we often take for granted is cherished by new immigrants to our country. Most of them understand that education is all-important, and therefore the teachers of their children are usually respected and even revered.

WHERE WE RANK

"What is honored in a country will be cultivated there."
— Plato

Occasionally we hear about data ranking the major industrialized nations in Reading, Math, and Science education. Many are shocked when rather than finding our country towards the top of the list we have to travel way down the list (depending on the year and the criteria) to (recently) 18th in Reading, 35th in Math, and 27th in Science. We often lament the "good old days" when things were different. Those days that I recall, that I experienced, education-wise, weren't all that great. Yes, we were expected to listen to the teacher, and would face the consequences at home if we didn't. But the methods, knowledge, research, resources available today, if utilized, are far superior to back then.

We teachers, every so often, are introduced to a pragmatic, profound way to teach math (no, not new math), a program which seems to benefit those with dyslexia, or a writing program which appears to work for the majority of the children. Whether these take too much time, effort, or get destroyed by the swinging pendulum, many of these exemplary programs seemingly disappear, get lost. Often, they are found by educational specialists in other countries who readily admit that they borrow their successful ideas from us.

I can count on one hand (two or three digits would suffice) the number of times that I, a teacher for 35 plus years, was asked for suggestions about improving education. Most of my responses were disregarded for various reasons, usually without an explanation. This book is a partial answer to that question for which I waited and waited. Who should one expect to know more about educating young children than those who are in the trenches, in the classroom, for six or seven hours a day, 185 days out of the year?

I believe that an overhaul, or even a tune-up to our educational system must begin with a renewed, regenerated, revived, a new-found RESPECT for education, educators, and a massive campaign which stresses the importance of a QUALITY education for EVERY individual, and how this will benefit both that person and society.

The deep bows, the heartfelt words of appreciation that we receive from many newcomers to this country, some who have emigrated from countries which have surpassed us in Math, Science, and Reading assessments, evaluations, continue to surprise the teachers who encounter them. These gestures reveal the value that these families place on education. The parents and grandparents eagerly tell you what they have sacrificed, are willing to sacrifice, for this treasured prize.

Hopefully, we will, before too long, get more than lip service from our congressmen and women, our state legislators.

"Your actions speak so loudly, I cannot hear what you are saying."
—Ralph Waldo Emerson

A BIG HINT: The answer is not MEGA-TESTING or SCRIPTED LESSONS. Those who are thinking in that direction might want to visit a REAL classroom.

In order to realize this dream, we must have a functional congress comprised of members who work together, get things done for the benefit of ALL of our citizens. Those who are an embarrassment, to our country or our intelligence, whether they pledge to block things from getting done, choose not to work with others, or fail to understand their oath of office, should be FIRED just like anyone else who is ineffective, incompetent or dangerous.

We must remove (almost) all the money from politics, elections. No one should be able to influence elections because of their wealth. A "rich" man's (woman's) vote should be worth no more than the poorest of the poor. Maybe then we could attract some good, decent, intelligent, passionate people with common sense who care more about policies and the people they are "representing," and less about the wishes of those who donate massive amounts of money to their re-election fund.

Maybe then we could engage young people, and increase the shamefully small percentage of the eligible electorate who vote, if they thought that their vote actually meant something.

The day teachers are paid a competitive starting salary, when EVERY child is valued and given whatever they need to succeed, necessary school funding is allocated automatically, when education is *actually* our **top priority**, then maybe there will be some movement northward in the rankings. More important, because of our enthusiasm, creativity, and superior education, we will be able to fill job openings with our well-prepared students. New jobs will be conceived and generated that never existed before, and we will be even more proud of ourselves and our country than ever before.

IMMIGRANTS

"I'd recognize that voice anywhere. It was the first kind voice I heard in America."

A former student who almost two decades earlier had been a new immigrant to our country.

The vast majority of us had ancestors who were once new immigrants to this country. Many of them came speaking little or no English. My father is first-generation (or second, depending on how this is defined) American, and even though he was born here in Chicago, when he began first grade at age six he did not yet speak English. (His mother arrived here already fluent in three languages).

Unfortunately, there are always some who make fun of others' accents, the grammar and cultural mistakes they make. Many young immigrants are ashamed of, embarrassed by their parents because they sometimes tend to stand out. WIBGI (Wouldn't it be great if) we took a small amount of time to learn a few common phrases in our new immigrant family's first language: "Good morning." "How are you?" "Thank you." "You're welcome." "Good-bye." That you are thoughtful enough to make the effort could make them feel more comfortable, accepted, as they strive to learn a new language (English), as well as the customs and laws of a strange, new land.

31 YOUNG PHILOSOPHERS

Looking for an honest, simple view of the world, a solution to a complex problem? Look no further than a young child who will cut through all the garbage to the basics, without biases. Here is some priceless wisdom gleaned from a how-to book dictated by kindergarteners:

How to Make A Tree House
First you look for a tree. Then put a floor on the tree. Staple the carpet down. Put the walls on. Put the top on. Put the door in and the window in. Fill the house up with the things and people that you love.

How to Fall Asleep
You lay down. Rest for a second. Then you fall asleep.

Most early childhood teachers can retell countless cute, clever, even profound statements made by their young students. The first one I recall hearing was told to me by a colleague, a kindergarten teacher. One of her former students, then my second grader, had the following one-sided conversation with her the morning following a back-to-school gathering. "Hey, Mrs. Hagar, I think I saw you last night, but then I thought, **MAYBE she has a twin sister!**"

While on yard duty, my first year of teaching, I was approached by a tearful, angelic first grader, *"Mr. Anderson, that big boy over there knocked me down!"* "I'm so sorry!" I replied. "Did he do it on purpose?" *"OH NO, MR. ANDERSON! He **meant** to do it ON AN ACCIDENT!"*

Many teachers entertain the idea of writing a book about the treasured comments they have compiled. I have tried to yield to them on this subject, but I had to sneak these in.

32 THE CHILDREN KNOW

Commuting on the brown line of the elevated train (the L) in my hometown, I spied a bit of tagging on the side of a building, **"THE CHILDREN KNOW!"** Yes, I reflected, they certainly do! I took another loop of the city in order to photograph the graffiti which would inspire me to write a book. The words spoke volumes to me.

THE CHILDREN KNOW intrinsically that "ALL MEN (women, and children) ARE CREATED EQUAL." They assume it and would not have any reason to believe that it should be otherwise. Soon, hopefully not too soon, they learn the sad truth, that this is not the way of the world.

Children know many things when they are young that they often forget on their way to becoming an adult. What your students soon know about YOU, their teacher, is if you care about them, if you respect them, if you mean what you say (Kids have a built-in balderdash detector), if they can trust you—if you even like them.

33 WORDS MATTER

Words matter! They can brighten one's day, or leave long-lasting, even permanent, gaping wounds. There are some phrases which can shorten or defuse arguments, conflicts, misunderstandings, and although they are often only a couple words in length, they are among the most difficult for many of us to say. "You're right!" "I'm wrong!" "I'm (so) sorry!"

Not only is it all right to make amends to a student or a class for things that you have done or said, it models for them how this could be done. "I shouldn't have said what I did." "It was wrong!" "I'm sorry!" "I'll try not to do it again!" "I apologize!" "I hope that you can forgive me!"

If I was aware that I had committed a transgression, I would apologize to the individual(s) in front of the other students, have a short discussion about what I did or said and why it was wrong or inappropriate. I would apologize again privately to them (probably outside), making sure that they understood that it was I who was wrong/out-of-line/rude, not them. I would give them the opportunity to respond, and make sure that they were ok before returning to the classroom.

For those who have trouble saying these and other simple but important words, "Thank you," "You're welcome," "I love you," if uttering them is painful, you might want to try something which has worked for me, practice saying them to a pet! (My dog appears to be receptive.) Eventually, one may be capable of communicating these important feelings to human beings. You may even save a relationship.

THE AVERAGE CLASS

School **should be** the **SAFE PLACE** for **ALL** children. For some it is a bubble from their other reality, a temporary escape where they can prosper, and obtain the skills and tools necessary to thrive in the world.

I recently had occasion to consult my binder of class photos. I was looking at pretty much an average class, in an average school in our district, which had limited bussing from an area with a relatively high percentage of "at risk" kids. I was reminiscing, and thinking how fortunate I was to be able to work with so many great kids, each with their unique story. As I perused the rows of children's portraits, I was struck by the number of "encumbrances" these kids had already accumulated by the age of seven or eight. It was amazing that some of them were able to function, let alone care about academics, or what this adult, their teacher, was jabbering, proselytizing about in the front of the room.

34 PEARLS OF WISDOM

BEWARE

Beware of white sugar, the north wind, and full moons, and plan accordingly, with alternate lessons in case they are needed.

WINK

Some kids feel invisible, and others occasionally need a little extra attention. Let them know that, even though you must spread yourself around, you are thinking of them, with a WINK, by touching their desk or their shoulder, somehow showing them that you care.

READY TO LEARN

One particular year, I had more than a handful of (capable) kids who often needed extra motivation to work. Before school one morning, I created a "boundary line" with one of our 12-foot jump ropes. As the children entered the classroom, I instructed them, "CROSS THIS LINE ONLY IF YOU ARE READY TO LEARN!" I left it up for a few days, until it had accomplished its desired goal and was no longer needed.

FRUSTRATIONS

You'll be frustrated often, by a child, parent, another teacher, your principal, or any number of things. In my personal experience, it was more often by someone or something in the "educational community," often to do with the latest fad, the "future of education," the latest swing of the pendulum. I recall conversing with a parent and her child that she was dropping off, who was noticing that I was lately getting more gray hairs. See what you kids are doing to Mr. A! I assured the child that it was not the kids, nor their parents that were causing the change in pigment, or the thinning of my mane, but rather it was those who are making the decisions in education. I earned each and every one of those graying and lost fibers.

My suggestion, if your job is secure, you have a trust fund, or like me, are stubborn (what I prefer to call "principled"), when the district or school administrator is pushing a new idea, consider it, and use it if it makes sense. If not, pretend to listen, and quickly lock your door! Keep the good stuff that works, despite what anyone else says, as long as it is LEGAL, BENEFICIAL TO THE KIDS, and NOT DANGEROUS. As a good friend and colleague reminded me often when I described a project I was contemplating, "It is (usually) easier to ask for forgiveness than to ask for permission."

SAVE

Save all of your annual class photos, and file them chronologically in a binder. Sounds simple, and obvious, right? While you are still teaching, you will often need to identify a child, recall the classmates of a visiting former student, what year they were in your room. Later, when your memory is not cooperating, and you're trying to remember one child out of the thousand or so students you've worked with, the photos, names, years, I assure you, will come in handy.

Treat yourself to a good quality bound book in which to jot down some of the funny, sad, outrageous, amazing, beautiful, profound statements, things, questions that your students said, did, and asked. You will cherish these later.

Keep a box in which to save some of the notes, including the thankful, grateful ones which you received from your students and parents. These will keep you going when the going gets tough as they are often the only encouragement that you will receive.

Later, you will enjoy reminiscing, smiling, giggling, and tearing up while perusing these mementos. Many of my friends and former colleagues now regret not having thought of this. When we are young and naïve we assume that our memories will always survive in our iron-clad minds. Wrong!

LAUGHTER

Most would agree that laughter is contagious. So is your mood, your attitude, your temperament. YOU determine the atmosphere in your classroom, whether it is WARM and WELCOMING, or it is TENSE and INDIFFERENT. Each classroom, and school, has its own personality, which one can feel when entering its space. Your kids pick up on your mood, so try to be "up" even if you don't feel at your best. If you are usually enthusiastic and have an occasional "down" day, the kids will forgive you. If you are upset, grumpy, sad, and feel like taking it out on the kids, don't. Instead, let them know that you're having a rough day. Show them that you are human. They will understand, support you, and respect you for it.

"A Giggle A Day Keeps The Gloomies Away."
Message on the first poster I ever displayed in my classroom

STRESS

Take care of yourself, whatever it takes, plenty of sleep, a healthy diet, exercise, a mini-vacation, yoga, tai chi, Pilates, meditation, walking, running, sports, dancing, reading, so that you can maintain your stamina, good attitude, and enthusiasm. This will ensure that you are able, to the best of your ability, to teach, take care of, and stand up for our kids.

STAY CURRENT

Stay current. Keep up with the times. Be familiar with the current music, people, jargon, sayings, etc. known to the kids. We had a bit of fun when we used popular (probably trademarked) logos for our classroom. NO FEAR, and LOCAL MOTION ("lifestyle clothing" brands) became NO EAR, the title of our bulletin board on Van Gogh, and LOCAL EMOTION, a title for our unit on local history.

A CLASS HANDSHAKE

You might build a bit of camaraderie with a CLASS HANDSHAKE, one which is used whenever you greet each other. This would include when you are welcoming your students first thing in the morning, setting the tone for the rest of the day. Collaborate with the children to create a handshake which is fun, but not so complicated that it cannot be remembered, or that it causes the line to get backed-up, wasting valuable class time.

Take risks, experiment!

Have the courage to say, "I don't know, good question! Let's find out!"

I believe, and tell the kids, A WISE PERSON LISTENS TO EVERYONE. You determine what you want to believe, what works for you.

Leave your EGO, your need for POWER, SARCASM, ANGST at the door.

If you're having a rough day, admit it to yourself and the kids. If you're not feeling that great about yourself, treat your kids how *you* would want to be treated, and you might be surprised with a boost in your own sense of self-worth.

35 CONTROVERSIES

CURSIVE

    I reflect on cursive only when I am scribbling my illegible signature, reading a historical document or a treasured handwritten letter from a friend or relative, doing a "copperplate" calligraphy project, or for the few weeks out of the year when I am instructing my students in the art of writing.

    Even though I personally choose to use a hybrid, slanted manuscript or bouncy italic hand, I hope that we maintain the practice of teaching cursive. For most of my children it was a source of joy and confidence building. I revealed to them my bias, what I held to be the truth, that second graders often scribed the most beautiful manuscript, and that hardly anyone's cursive could compare to that of a third-grader. I would suggest that we might want to challenge the sixth-graders to a cursive competition but would later renege, citing that we wouldn't want to embarrass them, or hurt their feelings. For that one year, when we were not that concerned with speed, the kids would produce writing which was worthy of framing. When we had learned all of the lower-case letters, my students enjoyed writing out (and memorizing the spelling of) the longest word in the English language.

pneumonoultra-
microscopicsilico-
volcanokoniosis

After we had added the upper-case (capital) letters to our achievements, we periodically played with abecedarian sentences, those which contained every letter of the alphabet.

> Acrobats excel with jumps and quick maneuvers
> on the flying trapeze.

Children should have at least a rudimentary knowledge of cursive so that they can read the written communication of their ancestors and historical documents. Whether they choose to continue with its use or prefer manuscript or italic script does not concern me, as long as they enjoy their choice, it fits their personality, and they can write legibly with a modicum of speed.

Many believe that, in the future, any form of handwriting will be superfluous because we will use our electronic devices for all of our writing needs. I pray that this is not the case. Though it's becoming a rarity, there is no better way of expressing one's thoughts, emotions, and creativity than in a hand-written letter. I take pleasure, savor, being the recipient of one in which the writer has obviously put some thought, care, and bit of their blood and soul down on paper.

WRITING IMPLEMENTS

If you notice that a student has an obvious problem with writing (forming letters), or that they are gripping their pencil so tightly that their fingers, hand, arm, and whole body are stressed, you will want to address the issue ASAP. Even before you determine a diagnosis, you might want to experiment with some optional writing implements. These are a few which have worked for many of my students (both righties and lefties).

"The Pencil Grip," which fits over pencils and crayons, encourages the child's fingers to grip the pencil (or other writing tool) correctly, and allows the fingers and hand to relax.

The "Twist 'n Write" pencil compels the user to hold the pencil correctly. They work so well that I would consider using them as an "introductory" pencil for young children.

The "Yoropen" (and for our kids, the Yoropen pencil) is reminiscent of the oblique pen holder (for those into calligraphy). It allows the writer to get a good view of what they are writing, and helps to alleviate the pressure and strain. This pencil is particularly beneficial for left-handed writers, and could solve problems such as smearing the letters which one has just produced.

Your left-handed writers will be appreciative if you are familiar with their unique issues. There are plenty of sites online which examine these. They will also be grateful if you are extra patient while they are finding a method which is comfortable and works for them.

HOMEWORK

As someone who had virtually no homework until high school, I contend that an *appropriate* amount of daily homework is extremely important. For the young child who is learning the basics of reading, math, and writing, extra practice is paramount to building a strong foundation. For learners through third grade, it is important to read to a parent (another adult or older child) for about 15 minutes daily. I found it beneficial to practice math for approximately the same amount of time, enough so the adult will be aware of the concept that you worked on in class, can check for understanding, and help right away if necessary.

Daily writing practice, possibly a short story or letter to a relative or friend is also helpful.

Each month I assigned a poem to memorize, plus a book report, each different and hopefully fun. All combined, if one was organized and without a learning challenge, the work should not have taken the child more than an hour. I also tried to give the kind of homework which would foster communication between the child and their family. I NEVER ASSIGNED BUSY WORK. If a parent wanted extra work for practice, I would recommend or lend them a supplementary book. If they were requesting work for baby-sitting or punishment, they would have to look for it elsewhere.

The children knew they wouldn't be getting out of the homework. Except in cases of illness, family crisis, or other emergencies, I expected the homework at the beginning of the day on the due date. Those who arrived without their daily homework, without an acceptable excuse, would complete that work at recess or some other time during the day.

What I never cultivated myself, which proved to be almost disastrous in college, was good study habits. Hopefully, this will not be a problem for my students.

TESTING

The most recent tragedy in education for young learners, in my view, is the trend of MEGA-TESTING. Without political lenses, this is what it looked like in reality at the third-grade level in our school district.

We first heard of this monumental change when large numbers of our administrators returned from a pilgrimage to a distant state, from which they would bring us word of the "future of education." Soon we gathered together and were told by our superintendent that we wouldn't be teaching anything but reading, math, and language arts (the subjects which would be tested on the new test), and that WE WOULD NOT BE TEACHING ART, MUSIC, SCIENCE, SOCIAL SCIENCE!"

Most of the primary teachers with whom I was acquainted complained about our new orders, and almost all followed them. Some courageous individuals snuck in a few art projects, but were ready with an explanation, argument, as to how these fit into the accepted standards. Then there were those who disregarded this directive, locked their doors and continued to provide a well-rounded curriculum. Some other districts interpreted the mandate more liberally (not meant in the political sense), and maintained what they knew worked for kids.

We were told which kids we "might want to" concentrate on, based on whether they could potentially raise our APY, a score which supposedly showed how well our school was doing, if our teachers and administrators were doing an acceptable job. This score could also be a factor in determining the real estate evaluation in a neighborhood/district, and thus where a parent might want their child to attend school, where they might want to live.

From the top down, pressure was applied. The superintendent, administrators, and teachers were concerned, worried, stressed, and one could feel the tension in the schools. Of course, this stress "trickled down" to the students. I recall well one first day of testing. Despite my efforts to assure the kids, "just do your best, you'll be surprised at how much you know, you're not expected to know everything, you'll do well…" and the prayers, meditation, deep breaths (whatever the children chose to de-stress), many children were visibly quite upset!

One child mumbled swear words and began to tear her test booklet. Another, an overwhelmed dyslexic who shouldn't have been taking the test without accommodations, was writing (in "mirror writing"), "HELP ME, HELP ME, HELP ME" on his test booklet. A third retched his last meal on the test. I cleaned off the vomitus as best I could, and calmed these three very bright students enough for them to proceed. In my A.D.D.-addled mind, I visualized the triptych which I would create for perhaps the office of the Secretary of Education from these test booklets, this trio of desecrated, sacred tests framed in red, white, and blue.

This is how the testing would go for the year (in third-grade, in our district). When we weren't actually TEACHING the children how to read, write, do math (and the plethora of other things a teacher is expected to do during the day), we would practice for the "benchmark" (a practice test which claimed to help prepare us for the test), take the benchmark, review the benchmark, with the kids, next with our teammates, and then with the principal (where our teaching abilities were sometimes questioned). This procedure would be repeated a couple more times before THE BIG DAY. Some have estimated that we were spending between 20 to 30 percent of our classroom time on testing — whatever percentage it was, it was way too much! Outside of class, teachers were required to spend hours of their time perusing the reports of the gathered statistics from each of these tests, time which took away from our planning for what we should have been doing to help those children who were "deficient" in basic areas, not to mention how this affected our own home lives.

My thoughts can be summed up by the pin (not necessarily worn, but appreciated by many of us):

CHOOSE (CIRCLE) THE CORRECT ANSWER:
TEST   TEACH

The kids would moan and groan each time I brought up the subject of testing. I empathized and sympathized, and made them a promise that I would spend only the absolute minimum amount required on testing. I can admit now that we would periodically (rather than using a shredder) have a bit of fun, relieve some frustration, by tearing up our practice tests, in half, again in half, until we couldn't tear the pieces any smaller. I also confess that once (or twice, possibly three times) I would bring shovels to class and allow volunteers, about 30 of them, to dig a large hole outside our classroom in which to bury the detritus of said practice tests for posterity. Maybe once (or twice) in lieu of the burial ritual, we may have snuck in an art project, perhaps stuffing Magritte-inspired clouds with the resultant scraps, decorated our bulletin board, and added an appropriate title, such as:

"Not Everything That Can Be Counted Matters,
And Not Everything That Matters Can Be Counted."
(I believe that Einstein said something similar to that).

I have known very few people who don't believe that children should be evaluated, although many disapprove of standardized tests. The extreme amount of testing that many of us observed, done at an age when we should be utilizing our precious time to make sure that all of our students are up to speed in the basics, is at best asinine, verging on criminal. I witnessed large numbers of second and third graders already burned-out, turned off, stressed, anxious because of the over-testing, and at the same time bored by the lack of a balanced curriculum.

Shortly after I quit my job to become a caregiver, I heard from several of my friends/colleagues. They called (individually), enthusiastically telling me that I would love this new philosophy! All of the kids will be learning the same basic things (standards). OK. Each teacher will determine, using their own style, personality, and strengths, how they will teach the concept. "It sounds like what you've always done," they declared! "YES, I believe that's what they call — **TEACHING!**"

Here is my idea of what an evaluation for first, second, and third graders should look like: First, decide what you want (expect) the kids to learn, for instance these math standards, these reading and language standards. Make this list of standards available to every child, parent, and interested member of the community. The parents, grand-parents, relatives, baby-sitter, whomever, could occasionally review the standards with the child and supplement the teacher's instruction with individual, practical, real world experiences. If a child continues to have difficulties with a particular standard, this should be communicated to the teacher by the parent.

Evaluate the children maybe once around the middle, and again towards the end of the school year. Test them on those standards which you told them were important to learn, using the same jargon, and the same format which was presented to them during instruction. Begin the test with some questions a grade level below so almost all will see some success. Proceed with grade level and some above-level questions, letting them know that there will be questions on the test that they're not expected to know. You will be able to ascertain if they learned what you told them was important for them to learn, you will have an idea where they are functioning, and you will have happier, better adjusted children. They won't be taking the SAT for about ten more years so there's plenty of time to gradually provide them with more challenging (and trick) questions.

If a child has learning challenges, provide them with accommodations such as extra time. If a child has a reading challenge, should we expect him/her to do "word problems" in math without accommodations? If we do, are we fairly evaluating their math skills?

Let's provide programs and evaluations which benefit our children (and our teachers), not those which make someone look good (or bad) at the expense of our children.

FACT OR OPINION

In the recent past, second and third-grade teachers were required, in one lesson, to teach our students the difference between a fact and an opinion. The children then completed a worksheet to prove their understanding of the concept. While teaching genres, we discuss fiction and non-fiction. It is now apparent that we need to introduce and stress the elements of exaggeration, fabrication, outright lies, propaganda, fake news, alternative facts and realities.   **SAD!**

CARE TOO MUCH

I've often been told that I CARE TOO MUCH, THAT I CAN'T SAVE EVERY CHILD. I'm not clear which kids they'd have me write off, which ones I should allow to fail. I do understand that I cannot "fix" everyone, solve all of their problems, or eliminate all their challenges.

What I can do, for the six hours I'm with them each school day, is to listen to them, and do everything I can to ensure that they have a successful academic and emotional experience for the one year they are in my class. I can help them prepare for whatever life has in store for them. I can try to treat them fairly, protect and defend them, and ignore any negative labels which have been affixed to them by others.

36 ACRONYMS

The following is a list of acronyms which might have been useful for this book:

OCNAYS	Of course, not at your school, your child's school, or the school you attended!
WIBGI	Wouldn't it be great if…
TOATP	Think of all the possibilities!
PSHAW	Yeh, right!
AYKM	Are you kidding me?
INKY	I'm not kidding you!
HINKY	Honestly, I'm not kidding you!

37 WOULDN'T IT BE GREAT IF (WIBGI)

A correspondent on a weekly "newsmagazine" program told us that a psychiatrist she knows asks every "client" the question, "When you were growing up, who loved you?" Unfortunately, many are not able to come up with a name. WOULDN'T IT BE GREAT IF **ALL** children and former children could (at least) respond with, "I know that all of my teachers **liked** me!"

FAVORITES

The discernable "disagreement" between the two girls was becoming a major disruption, so I approached them and motioned for them to step outside. I allowed them to stand on the bench so we would all see eye-to-eye. Then I flipped a coin to determine who would go first.

Girl #1: *"I'm your favorite, aren't I?"* "YES," I responded.

Girl #2: *"I thought that I was your favorite!"*

"You ARE!" I replied. "In my eyes, you are both tied for first!"

Occasionally, young kids will draw you pictures, write you notes, or come right out and voice that you are their favorite teacher. Usually, I just say, "THANK YOU." Sometimes I reply (and always think), "I hope that from now on, each (subsequent) teacher is your all-time favorite!"

38 SOME ENCOURAGING WORDS

Positive statements similar to these might help your students want to "keep up the good work":

Cool! Awesome! Sweet! ___!

Keep up the good work!

Very creative idea!

I liked what I saw you doing in class today, the way you ___!

I am so impressed that you ___!

You should be especially proud of yourself for ___!

You made my day! Thanks.

It wasn't easy to ___, but you did it!

You really persevered!

You're almost there!

If you need help, I'm here.

39 MARBLES

I've tried as a teacher to stay true to my values, philosophies, and principles (if not always to my principals). I have tried to incorporate my former career plans and interests into the classroom, my advocacy for women and girls (as well as boys), and while infusing art (including architecture) and music into the curriculum, I've been able to learn along with my kids. I did my best to ensure that my students wouldn't have the same negative experiences in the classroom or in the principal's office that I did, and that they'd have my ear. There was only one thing left on my list of ameliorating my early childhood grievances and perceived injustices.

During one of our discussions, my students inquired as to what I did at their age when I got bored. "Well, I began, you have to remember that this was a time before cable TV (we had maybe five or six stations); there were no personal computers, video games, or smartphones. In order to keep our mind occupied and stay out of trouble, we would, on the way to school, during recess, and on the walk home from school, play MARBLES!"

They were an awesome group (definitely tied for first), and whether they were just trying to please me, or were actually interested, they agreed unanimously that they wanted to try this. The following week they were educated on the basics, sat through demos of several marble games, shooting styles, after which I passed out the thirty-one baggies, each containing ten marbles.

Before we could begin playing, they would have to promise me that they were ok with the following rules, which they would copy off the board (handwriting practice), and return, signed by their parents:

Room 15 Marble Rules

1. Any marbles that can be seen or heard will be taken away.
2. You may bring up to 10 marbles to school.
3. When the bell rings, grab your marbles and get into line.
4. Marbles must be kept in some type of bag or container.
5. If a marble is dropped, it is picked up by the person who dropped it and given to Mr. Anderson.
6. Mr. Anderson does not want to hear about marbles during worktime.

Prior to assembling on the blacktop near the chalked-circles, I informed them that I would not be examining their hands or fingernails for tell-tale dirt, but when they entered the classroom after recess they were to line up at the sink and wash their hands.

Then, forming a huddle, we gave a short cheer.

40 ONE OF THE BIGGEST COMPLIMENTS

One of the biggest compliments you can receive as an educator is when a student refers to you as Mom or Grandma, Dad or Grandpa. When this happens, you can usually be assured that you've been accepted, that you are trusted as "one of the family."

41 WORLD'S GREATEST

On the last day of school, the children wrote their names on a small piece of paper, (literally) threw them into a hat, and then drew a name from the small heap. Without giving away who they had drawn, the kids thought about this person, their strengths, what positive things they were known for, what we would remember them for. They then created statues which symbolized this strength, trait, or achievement, using pencils, colored pencils, markers, and construction paper. In the last hour of the school year, we presented the awards to the recipients, **WORLD'S GREATEST** Mathematician, Reader, Scientist, Volleyball Player, Smile… Friend!

42 OTHER INSPIRATIONAL QUOTES

Show me, don't tell me. What kids might say if they were asked.

If it makes sense, look into it. If it works/will help a child (someone), use it. If it doesn't work, no matter who said it, ignore it.
— Carl David Anderson

(Use what talents you possess.) The woods would be very silent if no birds sang there except those who sang best.
— Henry Van Dyke

You can't always get what you want, but if you try sometimes, well, you might find you get what you need.
— Mick Jagger and Keith Richards

Ah, but I was so much older then, I'm younger than that now.
— Dylan

On teaching children—Do whatever necessary to ensure that they feel good about themselves. Help them, if needed, discover their strengths and talents, one or two things they are good at. Armed with self-esteem and confidence, in an environment of respect and trust, they will do their best, be happier, and have few, if any, behavior problems.
— Carl David Anderson

There is a voice that doesn't use words.   LISTEN
— Rumi

Life can only be understood backwards, but it must be lived forwards.
— Kierkegaard

To draw you must close your eyes and sing.
— Picasso

I don't understand a word you said, but I know exactly what you mean.
— Carl David Anderson

A girl's dreams are fragile, to be handled with care, for they largely determine, how the woman shall fare.

And perhaps I could have me a million more friends, and all I'd have to lose is my point of view.
— John Prine

STICK UP FOR KIDS—A "popsicle stick" quote, what remained of an ice cream bar which I had devoured. I later glued a pin to the back and wore it occasionally in class and around town.

Children may forget what you say, but they will never forget how you make them feel.
— Maya Angelou.

43 REFLECTIONS

While writing this book, I had an opportunity to reminisce, to reflect on my years in education, revisit notes from students and their parents, my class pictures and each child's unique story. I realize now more than ever how fortunate I have been to be able to spend so much of my life with young children. I was energized every day by their fresh, unbiased view of the world, the joy they exuded when learning something new, their curiosity, sense of fairness, and simple, common sense solutions to seemingly complex problems. I didn't fully appreciate how spoiled I was until I left their world to join what most face each day, an often divisive, unfair, irrational reality created by adults.

Kids frequently asked me, "DO YOU LIKE BEING A TEACHER?" I told them the truth, "I LOVE WORKING WITH YOU KIDS!"

Teaching young children… It may not have been what I envisioned, what I planned to do, but I'm pretty sure that IT WAS WHAT I WAS MEANT TO DO!

HOPE

Hope is the thing with feathers
That perches in the soul,
And sings the tune without the words,
And never stops at all.

And sweetest in the gale is heard;
And sore must be the storm
That could abash the little bird
That kept so many warm.

I've heard it in the chilliest land,
And on the strangest sea;
Yet, never, in extremity
It asked a crumb of me.

Emily Dickinson

44 CAUTION!

I leave you with this thought. We may not always listen to kids, but they DO listen to us. Walking to my classroom one morning, I heard a voice from the past, one which I easily retrieved from that special place in the brain where fond memories are stored.

"Mr. A?" asked the voice.

"MAYA!" I exclaimed, turning to see a young woman, now about 15 years older and two feet taller, but unquestionably Maya, my former second grader!

After a hug, I queried, "What are you doing here, Maya?"

She explained that she had just graduated from college, and was taking a break, to work with kids, UNTIL SHE STARTED MED SCHOOL!

I couldn't have been more proud of her!

"MAYA, YOU DID IT!"

"You said I could!" she replied.

ESSENCE

I give you the books I've made,
Body and soul, bled and flayed.
Yet the essence they contain
In one poem is made plain,
In one poem is made clear:
On this earth, though far or near
Without love, there's only fear

ACKNOWLEDGEMENTS

I am eternally grateful to:

Miss Mary Martin for your unconditional support, whether it was comforting me and allaying my concern that I was wrong or crazy just because I was the only staff member with a particular view—talking me through some tough times—gently, but firmly, urging me to write this book, or for taking the time to "simply" listen. For all you've done for my kids, there will always be a place reserved for you in my heart. This is your book too, Miss Mary, for without your involvement, this story would be incomplete. If only everyone could be so fortunate to have a friend like you!

My friend B, who was sent my way just in time to help with this book. After untold hours of labor, you succeeded in transforming my random collection of Word files into something one can now recognize as a book. Without your assistance, your devotion, my words and thoughts may have remained imprisoned in some electronic file, or lost on some far-off cloud, for eternity.

Andrew Benzie, my creative, patient publisher, who made this final stage of the process a fun, positive learning experience.

My family and friends for your understanding and support.

KE for being my trusted guide in the book world.

CL, VB, KR, and MG for generously sharing your ideas.

KS for your wisdom, friendship, and for being a good listener.

DS for early morning discussions, critiques, and for helping me appreciate the thought processes of a younger generation.

SK for your thoughts and editing skills… and for providing sustenance for three generations of my loved ones.

SJ who sifted through my manuscript, offering suggestions while remaining a good neighbor.

D, my reflection, my "mirror," for keeping me (relatively) sane and functional.

Lastly, I want to acknowledge and salute the dedicated, caring teachers who daily, without any fanfare, give their all to educate EVERY child entrusted to their care.

ABOUT THE AUTHOR

Carl David Anderson is not a best-selling author, and he assures us that LISTEN TO ME: A Child's Plea is the last book which will bear his name. Once he was able to figure out how his own mind processed words and symbols, he gained a passion for reading and a reverence for books, especially hand-made, hand-written and illustrated ones, such as those created by his students. Although his brain has generated many "mind books" over the years, this is his first published book. He hopes that it will be a good vehicle for assisting a new generation of teachers in providing young children with a solid educational and emotional foundation. Mr. Anderson taught and was an advocate for first, second, and third-graders for about 35 years.

www.ingramcontent.com/pod-product-compliance
Lightning Source LLC
Chambersburg PA
CBHW032107090426
42743CB00007B/265